THE BLOOD THE FIRE
AND THE SWORD

THE BLOOD THE FIRE AND THE SWORD

Patricia Eze

authorHOUSE®

AuthorHouse™
1663 Liberty Drive
Bloomington, IN 47403
www.authorhouse.com
Phone: 1-800-839-8640

This book is based on real life events. The real names of people involved have been changed to protect their privacy.

All Bible quotes in this book are taken from the King James Version (KJV) and the New International Version (NIV).

Published by AuthorHouse   07/12/2012

ISBN: 978-1-4772-1545-6 (sc)
ISBN: 978-1-4772-1546-3 (hc)
ISBN: 978-1-4772-1547-0 (e)

Any people depicted in stock imagery provided by Thinkstock are models, and such images are being used for illustrative purposes only.
Certain stock imagery © Thinkstock.

This book is printed on acid-free paper.

CONTENTS

This book is dedicated to my closest friend, my harshest critic, my most precious and dearest love—my husband, Patrick. Your deep and unswerving faith in our Lord has helped to keep me grounded and focused on the cross of Calvary and has challenged me into wanting to strive for excellence in everything that I do. This is also for my two children, Richaida and Rueben, who are my heartbeat and inspiration. I pray you will both continue to grow in God's grace.

PSALM 27

The LORD is my light and my salvation; whom shall I fear? The LORD is the strength of my life; of whom shall I be afraid? **2** When the wicked, even mine enemies and my foes, came upon me to eat up my flesh, they stumbled and fell. **3** Though an host should encamp against me, my heart shall not fear: though war should rise against me, in this will I be confident. **4** One thing have I desired of the LORD, that will I seek after; that I may dwell in the house of the LORD all the days of my life, to behold the beauty of the LORD, and to enquire in his temple. **5** For in the time of trouble he shall hide me in his pavilion: in the secret of his tabernacle shall he hide me; he shall set me up upon a rock. **6** And now shall mine head be lifted up above mine enemies round about me: therefore will I offer in his tabernacle sacrifices of joy; I will sing, yea, I will sing praises unto the LORD.

CHAPTER 1

Searching

It all started one Thursday afternoon in October 2001 on the Caribbean Island of Saint Lucia where I had been living for the past five years. A friend of mine had invited me to a lunchtime prayer session at a local church, and I had not hesitated to accept, as I liked anything to do with the Church and the Lord Jesus.

I had never been to Bethel Tabernacle Church before; in fact, I don't even think I had even heard of the name. I had been a baptised Seventh Day Adventist nine years before, and I remember that a great deal of fuss was made because both my husband Marius and I had been baptised together, and this in itself was probably quite a rare thing.

The afternoon meeting started promptly at 12.30, and there were probably only about thirty people in attendance all scattered throughout the pews. My friend, who was named Barbara, advised me to sit in the second aisle toward the front so that we could get prayed for quickly and then shoot off back to work.

As I sat down, I faced the front of the church where a thick-set, middle-aged woman stood at a Perspex podium reading and speaking to the people in attendance. When she had finished speaking, she started to sing worship songs, and encouraged us to praise God and open ourselves up to the spirit of the Lord. I looked around the church, and noticed that mostly women were present. The songs they were singing were new to me, and had a jaunty Pentecostal feel to them as opposed to some of the songs that I was used to singing at my local church. There was no musical accompaniment, but on the podium a set of shiny red drums and a keyboard piano stood idle.

After a while, a tall, dark-skinned gentleman appeared from an entrance towards the front right-hand side of the church. He took a seat on the first bench next to some other people, and shortly after this, the praise and worship singing came to an end. The woman who was officiating welcomed the gentleman who I later found out was a deliverance minister. The minister welcomed everyone to the service and began to talk to the people who were sitting in the pews about a book, which he had in his possession, that detailed pictures and symbols of a demonic nature. He said that we should go home and discard any items we may have in our possession that bore any similar logos. The minister then led us in a prayer that we repeated after him asking for the forgiveness of the Lord for sins we had committed in the past. In addition to this, he prayed and asked the Lord to break generational curses and soul ties, but quite frankly at that point in time I didn't have a clue what he was talking about.

After the prayer was finished, we were invited to write our prayer requests on a special form and drop it in the offering basket with an offering. The principle behind giving the offering and making a prayer request is that you must sow a seed, or make a sacrifice to God, which is a sign of your faith in him, and in return you should wait upon him for a blessing. These principles are clearly outlined in the Bible in the book of Malachi, where the prophet speaks about tithing to the Lord and reaping the blessings that are promised in return for your obedience to God's word. After the offering was collected, a man and a woman joined the minister and took up positions on either side of him. The lady next to him held a small bottle in her hands, which I later found out contained olive oil. The other gentleman stood a little distance apart and spoke quietly to himself. The minister then invited people seated in the pews to approach him and form a line. He asked everyone to allow those who needed to return to work to be prayed for first. My friend Barbara hastily pushed me forward, telling me to hurry up, and I actually ended up being first in the queue.

I soon realized that the minister was staring at me, and I felt a little uncomfortable and began to smile nervously. The minister asked me to move forward and stand nearer to him. I soon found myself standing directly in front of him. All the while he refused to take his eyes off me, making me feel as if he was looking straight through me. 'Hello, my sister, how are you?' he asked.

'Oh, I'm fine thank you!' I answered, but he kept staring at me, and I became increasingly uncomfortable.

'My sister, I can see that you are carrying a very heavy load! I can see that you love the Lord, but you are being prevented from serving him as you need to because of this heavy load!' I smiled at the man sheepishly, thinking that he was referring to my husband and the marital difficulties that we were having, so I told him that he was right. He then replied that he was going to pray for me so that the Lord would release me from the suffering and bondage that I was experiencing. I closed my eyes and bowed my head in agreement, as the minister took my hand.

The minister then proceeded to pray in a very strong and authoritative voice, and as he did so, he gently squeezed my hand. I remember that he specifically said that he was coming against all demonic activity and generational curses that had come into my life. He prayed and asked the Lord to close all doorways in my life that had allowed the demonic infestation to take place, and he also asked the Lord to bind up the strong man on my behalf. During this time, I was wondering what was going on, because his grip on my hand had become increasingly firm. 'In the name of Jesus Christ of Nazareth, come out of her now! I command you, devil, to loose your hold on this woman right now! Let her go!'

Well, up to that point I thought that things were a little odd, but I kept my eyes closed anyway and tried to concentrate on being prayed for. However, nothing could have prepared me for what happened next. As the man's voice became increasingly fervent, and his grip on my hand tightened even more, I experienced a very strange sensation. All of a sudden, the minister touched my forehead with oil from the bottle that the lady standing next to him held in her hand. I felt weak at the knees. My knees buckled underneath me, and I collapsed to the floor in a semiconscious state.

I felt myself on the floor, and I was aware that people were near me. I could not open my eyes because they felt as if they were glued shut. At first I was unable to move, but then after a while I felt my body begin to jerk in different directions. I began to writhe and twist on the floor, and then I felt someone pinning my legs and my arms to the ground.

'In the name of Jesus, get out of her!' *Is this me?* I wondered if they were talking to me. *Who are these people? What is happening, and what are they doing? Why am I on the floor, and why am I shaking like this? I want to go back to my office*, I thought to myself, and I was clueless about the length of time that I actually spent on the floor. After a while, I realized that I had stopped shaking and I was able to open my eyes. I noticed that there were two ladies kneeling right next to me. One of the ladies kindly helped me to my feet and smoothed out my ruffled hair so that it didn't look as though I had just woken up. I looked around and I noticed that most of the people who had been in the congregation had already left.

I must have been on the ground for well over an hour, and I sat down on a nearby bench wondering about what had just taken place. My friend Barbara must have already left to return to her office, and I had now become very late for work. As I sat on the bench, I tried to compose myself as best I could, but I knew that something very peculiar had just happened to me, and I had to find out what it was. As I walked out of the church, I noticed that there was something physically different about me. I felt as though a part of me was gone. I felt empty, and even light headed. To be honest, I really didn't know what to think. I felt totally confused, and still slightly dazed. I wondered why I had fallen on the floor like that, and also why I hadn't been able to get up when I wanted to.

As I returned to my office and sat at my desk, there were lots of questions going round and round in my head, and I now had to search for someone to give me the answers. I picked up the phone directory and searched the yellow pages for the listing of churches. A chord of excitement flowed through me when my eyes saw the entry that I was searching for.

Bethel Tabernacle Church, Sans Soucis, Castries.

I hurriedly dialled the number, and soon I was speaking to the secretary asking her if I could speak to the tall, dark gentleman who had been in the church praying for people. 'I'm sorry, Minister Williams is still in deliverance, can I take a message please?' I thought for a moment whilst wondering what deliverance was. I confirmed that I did want to leave a message, and the secretary wrote down my name and telephone number so that the minister could return my call. 'Hello?' I said, hoping to catch her before she hung up. 'What did you say his name was again? I mean the name of the man in deliverance?' The secretary replied that the man's name was Minister Nathaniel Williams, and that she would give him my message as soon as he had finished working in the church.

I replaced the receiver and allowed my mind to drift. I felt so strange. Something had definitely left me, but I couldn't put my finger on it. I tried to concentrate on doing some work that afternoon, but it was near enough impossible.

I had hardly paid any attention to my assistant Dawn, who sat idly by her desk. I looked at her and wondered if she could tell if there was anything different about me . . .

CHAPTER 2

Knowledge Is Power

My mind wandered and wandered, and I felt uncomfortable as I was in totally unfamiliar territory. Suddenly the phone rang and it startled me out of the faraway place in which I had found myself. 'Hello,' said a deep male voice, 'this is Nathaniel Williams, can I speak to Hannah please?'

'Oh yes, this is she speaking!' I proceeded to thank him for returning my call and also for seeing me that afternoon. I told him that I would very much like an explanation of what had happened to me that day because I had been feeling very strange after leaving the church. It was as if there was a new, empty place inside me that I couldn't really explain. Minister Williams laughed and tried to explain that I had been demonized. He assured me that some of the demons had left me. I sat at my desk in complete shock and disbelief. I told him that he must be mistaken as I was a born-again Christian and had been serving God properly. There was no way that what he was saying could be true.

I asked why I had been jerking around on the floor and why I hadn't been able to get up when I wanted to. He then went onto explain that demons could control the body but not the soul of a Christian, and that infestation is still possible. I really didn't understand a word he was saying, and he must have sensed from my tone that I was getting a little annoyed. He informed me that perhaps it would be better if I made an appointment to see the pastor of the church, and I agreed. He advised me that the pastor was currently on vacation and would be back in a couple of weeks' time. This was very disappointing to me as I needed answers immediately, and I was feeling totally confused. I made an appointment anyway, but also asked if it would be possible to see him again as there were still many questions that I had to have answered.

I kept the appointment with Minister Williams a couple of days later, but to be honest I was still determined to see the pastor himself, as I hoped he could give me some more information about my unfortunate predicament. On the day of the appointment with the pastor, the secretary showed me into his office. He greeted me with a large, warm smile and a very strong handshake. 'Good afternoon, my dear lady, and how are you doing today?' Without waiting for an answer, he explained that his name was Pastor McLorren and that he was the pastor of the Bethel Tabernacle Church. I introduced myself to him, and then he proceeded to ask me what he could do for me. I began to tell him of my encounter a few weeks before with Minister Williams. Pastor Mc Lorren asked me many probing questions about my family and my parents, where I lived, and where I was from. The questions seemed never ending and very personal. I opened up as honestly as I could because I was desperate to get to the bottom of all of the drama.

I explained that I came from a Christian background and that I was a practising Seventh Day Adventist. I explained that I was in an abusive relationship with my husband and that my father had recently died. I also informed him that I had come back from visiting my mother in Jamaica about a year before with my two small children and at that time, I had started having some very strange experiences and bad dreams. He asked me to explain some of the dreams that I had been having, and then asked me if there were any more strange experiences that I would like to mention. When I started talking about experiences that I had had over the years, I realized that there were more than I really cared to admit. I had locked most of the stories away in the hidden vaults of my subconscious mind and was able to bring them to the surface only once Pastor McLorren asked certain specific questions of me. He listened to me carefully, and at times I noticed that he raised his eyebrows and punctuated my storytelling with little exclamations of what seemed like a combination of concern and surprise. I wanted to know what Minister Williams had meant when he said that I had been demonized and that some of them had left me. How many of them did I have? I had been a Christian all of my life, and I was sure that there must have been some mistake.

Finding the answers to all of my questions took me on a long journey of self-discovery and spiritual research that I believed would be ongoing. I really doubt if anyone truly has all of the answers to what goes on in the unseen world. Pastor McLorren asked me if it would be possible for me to bring my husband to his office so that he could meet him, and I thought long and hard about this question before I was able to answer. I told him that I would probably have to make up some excuse as he did not attend 'Sunday church', and I didn't know if he would even entertain the idea of entering a church on any other day either. The secretary made another appointment for me and my husband to attend another session. Marius consented to go to the meeting after I explained that there could be an opportunity for him to get some new painting and decorating work, as he was a private contractor. I had hoped that I was not stretching the truth too far, but I knew that the only thing that might motivate him to attend the appointment was if he thought that there was something in it for him.

On the morning of the next appointment I noticed that Pastor was sitting behind his desk but there was another lady also present who sat on the couch on the opposite side of the room. We were introduced to this lady as Sister Jenny. As she sat quietly throughout the whole appointment, she appeared to be taking notes of what was being said. We spoke at length, and Pastor counselled and explained, mediated, questioned, and then finally prayed. Pastor said that I was suffering from a generational curse and that being a Christian would not automatically exempt me from this. He explained that being demon possessed means that a person has absolutely no functional control over his or her body, mind, or soul *at any time*. The condition is not the same as demonization which is much less severe. The pastor referred me to Mathew, chapter 8, which describes the behaviour of two men who were totally possessed by devils. The minds and bodies of those who are demonized may be temporarily affected but never their souls. Thus a child of God can be demonized but not demon possessed.

I was told that I had to renounce all generational curses and soul ties and that I had to undertake a few sessions of deliverance prayers to be free from the yoke that I had found myself in. *More mumbo jumbo*, I thought to myself, *but what if I really am cursed, and what if it could affect my children?* Pastor McLorren then asked me if I was ready to be prayed for right there and then, and I replied that I was. He started off by saying that I should not get nervous and that we were going to hold hands. He said that firstly I should repeat a prayer of renunciation after him, and then after that he was going to pray for me.

I soon found myself on the floor again, writhing and kicking and punching, yawning and coughing. I was aware that other people had come into the room, and they were holding my legs and arms firmly down to the ground. The grip on my arms and legs were so tight that I almost felt that the blood was being prevented from running through my veins. Someone was also holding my head in place because I was banging it on the ground, and although I knew it was painful, I did not know how to stop myself from doing it. People were all around me in the room, and although I could see them, my mind's eye imagined them as if they were in abstract. I was no longer speaking quietly and respectfully to the pastor, but I could hear myself uttering profanities and hitting out and spitting whenever I could work myself loose.

'You foul spirit of violence, come out of this woman now! I command you in the name of Jesus Christ of Nazareth to come out of her! Now, Satan, it is written that I have power over you and over all of your works, and so I have taken my rightful place in the third heavens with my Master and I am coming against you with the precious blood of my Lord and Saviour Jesus Christ! By the power that has been invested in me, I bind you and cast you out and order you to return to the abyss now!' Pastor and the team sang and prayed and intermittently gave commands to the devils to leave my body. Although I was cognizant

11

of and could remember some of things that happened to me, I was not conscious of all of them, and I especially had no idea of time. During the deliverance session, pastor called and listed the names of different spirits and commanded them to leave my body, and upon hearing certain names I would jerk about with more intensity and fury, and this would make the people in the room pray harder and call for the Holy Ghost fire from heaven to seek out and burn the spirit that was manifesting at that time. When it was over, I noticed that I had been 'away' for more than two hours, and that I had been to a faraway place of which I knew nothing. Although my eyes were shut, I had seen a goat wearing a crown on his head and a purple cape around his shoulders and fierce-looking monsters with jagged, stained teeth roaring at me.

I was completely physically drained by the time I came around, and it took me some minutes to gather my thoughts as I was helped up from the floor onto the couch. I felt so incredibly embarrassed as I realized what had happened and that the eyes of everyone in the room had been upon me. Several people asked me how I was feeling. Someone asked if I wanted some cold water to drink, and I accepted the kind offer because my throat was by then feeling so sore because I had been shouting and screaming so intensely during the previous moments. The secretary gave me another appointment to come back to see the pastor in his office the following week. Before I left, the pastor told me about the dangers of opening the door of my soul to the enemy again. He warned me to keep myself pure and holy and to not to get angry. He asked me if I had ever heard about or read the books of Rebecca Brown, and when I responded that I hadn't, he gave me one and instructed that

I read both it and my Bible and engage in as much prayer and worship of the Lord as possible.

Marius took me home that afternoon but never said a word to me. My mind was in a complete whirl, and everything that I had known before to be true no longer made any sense. All of the goal posts had changed, and I felt lost and humbled. I felt a strong urge to seek the face of God as I never before had done, and I was sure that he was the only one who could help me out of this awful situation.

I found myself attending deliverance services every Thursday afternoon so that I could be prayed for so that the remaining demons could be cast out. I also attended Sunday morning services both at 7.30 and 10.30 because I wanted to be in the presence of God where I felt safe and empowered. I had been and still was officially a Seventh Day Adventist and knew about the importance of keeping the Sabbath day holy. I also believed that to break the Sabbath was to condemn one's soul to eternal damnation and hellfire, and so I decided to attend both churches just to be on the safe side. I knew that it all sounded silly, but what else could I do? I believed in the Sabbath teachings, but had always had a problem with the incorporation of the supplementary teachings outside the Bible, including the adoration of the writings and thoughts of Ellen G. White and others, which I personally thought were irrelevant to my Christian walk with God. I always disputed why the Bible alone could not be enough as a guide and way of life for a born-again believer, and felt that it was erroneous to rely on anything else because it might alter or dilute the true word of God.

As the months rolled by, I stayed at home with the children and sang and prayed and played worship music all day long, always trying to find peace within my soul. I continued to get counselling and prayer from Pastor McLorren and his team, and I slowly began to mature and become more cognizant of the things that are not seen but are discerned by the Spirit of God.

It was about this time that I realized that I was not sleeping well in the house anymore and that there were occasions when I would wake up to find long scratches on my chest and back. At other times, I would wake up to excruciating pains in my tummy, which would then wear off as the morning rolled on. These pains did not coincide with my menstrual cycle and were otherwise unexplainable. One day I mentioned these scratches and pains to Marius, who said that it sounded as if I was being attacked by *magie noire*, or in other words, an agent of black magic that operated in the night to sexually attack women. Again, I didn't have a clue about what he was talking about. It seemed like more hocus-pocus to me, and I wasn't particularly interested. However, the attacks continued and the scratches persisted on my chest and back.

Again I mentioned the matter to Marius and he stated that he was going to take me to his grandfather for treatment and prayers. He said that his grandfather was a good man and was always able to help people when they had problems. Mr. Joseph was not his real biological grandfather, but an old family friend. Marius took me to his house, which was about three miles or so away from where we lived. The house was situated on many acres of land and had been constructed of wood many, many years before. The outside of the house was overrun by scores of ducks, which roamed free. There were droppings everywhere. Upon entering the house, I noticed that most of the floorboards had completely rotted and that there were big lizards, cockroaches, and ants everywhere. Mr Joseph asked me to sit down, and I picked my way through the room until I found a rusty, metal-framed chair with a worn and flat cushion resting on the seat. Marius explained to Mr Joseph what my problem was, and he agreed to help me. He instructed me to come back early the next morning to take him to get the medicine that he would need to do the prayers for me.

The next morning I woke up bright and early after another hard night and set out to fetch Mr Joseph. He made me drive him all the way to Gros Islet, which is a few miles north of Castries where I lived, and stop the car in front of a particular tree. I got out of the car and watched him as he selected leaves from it. He stated that he was looking for the male and female parts of the tree, as these were needed to make the medicine. I just went along with this scene, totally not understanding the consequences of what I was participating in or what was actually happening. After I dropped Mr Joseph home again, he promised to come to my house later that evening, which he did. He brought leaves and twigs that he'd bound with string into multiple bundles. These, he said, I was to place on top of the frame of every window and door in the house in order to keep the bad spirits away. He also gave me a prayer to read and some incense to burn every night before six o'clock.

I complied with this ritual every evening as instructed, but got absolutely no relief from the attacks. One day I decided to take a closer look at the prayer that I had been reading, and noted that it mentioned the great master of the universe and things of that nature. I paused for a moment and reflected on this. I soon realized that these prayers and incense and twigs by the windows and doors were a load of rubbish and were not helping me at all. In fact, if anything, the problems that I was experiencing seemed to be getting worse, and so I decided to remove the twigs and throw away the incense and the piece of paper on which the prayer was written. During one of my Thursday sessions at the church, I mentioned these things to the pastor. He advised me that demon forces were, in fact, attacking me, and that the latest paraphernalia brought into my house would only attract more of them. He was pleased that I had listened to the voice of the Holy Spirit and gotten rid of them. The spirits that had formerly visited my house were only replaced by stronger and more dangerous ones, and that is why I was still experiencing the problems.

CHAPTER 3

A New Beginning

Handy Construction Ltd was owned by Burt Davies, a tall, stocky man in his late thirties. Burt had a bald head and wore lots of gold chains around his neck and also around his wrists. He was a self-made businessman who dabbled in the construction and renovation of buildings, along with car sales. He had also even been a restaurateur at one point in time.

Marius, my husband, brought Burt home to meet me one day. At the time Marius and I had recently returned from living and working in the United Kingdom, and I was working from home as a freelance real estate agent. I answered the door when I heard my husband outside calling me. I clearly remember that I was trying to make myself some letterhead stationery that I could use for my business, which I had decided to call Helen Estates Realtors. Although I had used a computer for years, I was mostly familiar with data input, and I found that creating documents was much more challenging. For that reason, the interruption at the door came as a welcome break.

'Hello, my name is Burt, and you must be Hannah!' The man stood at the door with a wide, beaming grin on his face as he stretched his right hand towards me. 'Marius was telling me earlier that you were into real estate,' he continued as I ushered him inside, 'and I thought that perhaps we could talk to see if we could help one another. He told me that you're working from home, and I know that can have its drawbacks.' I chuckled at this, and agreed with Burt by nodding my head. Indeed, working from home might at first glance appear to be a very good alternative to facing the traffic and the hustle and bustle of the commute to and from work, but then this has to be weighed against being expected to still do the cooking, cleaning, and ironing, looking after the kids, and doing all of the other household chores in between. I thought that at least if I was out at work, I could focus on getting my business off the ground. There would not be the interruptions of loud music blaring from neighbours' houses, or having to hang clothes out on the washing line, or gather them in again if it started to drizzle with rain. I thought that these things amounted to additional pressures, but the truth of it probably was that whichever way you looked at it, women have the short end of the straw no matter how they juggle home and work.

Burt then proceeded to offer me a partnership in his business and explained that he knew lots of people who were building homes for rent or sale, and that he could give me many contacts in that area. He proposed that we should share the profits equally. He would give me the names and contact information of people who wanted the service of a real estate agent, and I would then give him half of the profits that the business made. He said that I could share his office and make use of Dawn, his secretary, who didn't have very much to do anyway. There

18

would be no cost to me, and I could run the business however I saw fit. Burt even promised to pay me a salary because he acknowledged that it might be some time before I made the first sales, and he knew that, in the meantime, I would need some money for subsistence.

The proposal sounded wonderful—almost too good to be true. After our conversation, I returned to my computer feeling elated at the prospect that I would be given such assistance in my business. When I thought about it, I knew that it was pointless inf being a real estate agent if I didn't know anyone who had any property to sell or anyone who wanted to buy anything.

At the beginning of the following week, I moved my computer and office equipment from the house to my new office, which was in the city of Castries. The office was of a reasonable size and it also had a small interior office where Burt kept his books, laptop computer, and various drawings of house plans. I was very excited about having my own business, because I had always thought that I had the capability to make such a venture work. I had spent all of my working life in the UK working for local authorities or housing associations, and I had even gone to university to study about building technology, the history of social housing, and business law. I had been dealing with people and their housing problems for years. I have seen live mushrooms growing out of kitchen walls due to seriously damp conditions, and I have seen cockroach infestations so bad that they actually lived inside refrigerators and fell from the ceiling into open pots of food on the stove.

Life for me at the time was very hard, and I felt that I was trapped in a loveless marriage. Marius and I met for the first time when he appeared

on my doorstep one afternoon in London, England, in 1991. It turned
out that he had been watching me and waiting for my return from
work for a few days. He knocked on my door and explained that he
was staying just a few houses away with his brother and his family. He
handed me a note and explained that he had been about to leave it on
my car but then decided not to as he realized that I would not know
who it was from. Rather, he had opted to wait until I arrived home to
hand deliver it instead.

I refused his request to come into my house, and also to give him
my phone number, but I took the note from his hand anyway whilst
smiling and feeling very pleased with myself. *What a cute guy*, I thought
as I climbed the stairs to the first-floor apartment, which I had been
occupying alone since I moved there a few years before. I had purchased
the property when I was just twenty-one years old because my parents
had emigrated to Jamaica in 1987 after my father's retirement. I lived
alone but had some good friends who made life worthwhile. I was
twenty-six years old and had no boyfriend, so the prospect of a really
handsome guy such as the one who had just showed up at my door
pleased me greatly.

What followed in the coming days can only be described either as
harassment or very intense courting. The warm, exciting feeling of being
chased by a prospective suitor gave way to irritation. At times I even
felt as though I was being stalked. I soon dreaded coming home in the
evening for fear that Marius would be lurking around waiting for me as
was his practice. No sooner would I arrive home than I would hear my
doorbell ringing. He would be standing there with a big, cheesy grin
on his face asking for me to let him in. The conversation at first could

be described as inquisitional on my part, as I wanted to find out as much about him as possible. He told me that he was a chef and that he had been living and working in the French Caribbean island of Tortola, a place that I had never heard of before. He told me that he possessed his own house and vehicle and was doing very well for himself, but it was not until some months later that I found out that these details were untrue. Marius stated that his brother had asked him to come to England on holiday as a thank you for all of the kindness he had shown to him in the past, as he had constructed his house for him.

Over the course of the coming weeks, Marius told me all sorts of weird and colourful stories about himself to win over what he obviously thought was a good catch—a single professional woman with no children, with her own place, her own car, and her own money, with a free entry pass to the UK. However, there was something about him that I just didn't like, and it was a source of irritation to me. He presented himself as being so polite and longsuffering and tolerant of the insults that I started to hurl his way. *Why can't he be a man and toughen up a bit and at least answer me back or defend himself?* I wondered.

At one point I stopped letting him in because I felt that he was crowding my space. He wanted to come over every day, but I needed my privacy and space with my friends. Intellectually speaking, I found him to be limited, and although he was good looking, which was a bonus, I did not know if I would be able to cope with him. I remember asking him one day what version of the Bible he would buy if he needed one. Well, his response surprised me even though I had worked out for myself that he wasn't very well educated. I ended up asking the question in no less than half a dozen different ways before I was able to extract his final answer, which turned out to be 'The Holy Bible'. I asked him if he had ever heard of the King James, New King James, or New International versions. From the look on his face, I knew that I was flogging a dead horse.

One rainy and cold Saturday evening I was at home alone listening to music when I heard my doorbell ring. I wondered who it could be as I walked down the stairs. I opened my apartment door and walked into the hallway toward the communal door, which was shared by myself and my neighbour, Carol, who lived in the downstairs apartment with her daughter, Karina, who was about ten years old at the time. I shouted through the door asking the person to identify himself, and a familiar but unwelcome voice answered, 'It's me, Marius.' My heart dropped. *Oh, not again*, I thought. I shouted back asking him what he wanted, and he replied that he wanted to see me and to come in. I paused for a while and then answered that I was busy. This led him to plead with me through the glass-panelled door for what seemed like an eternity. I then supposed that it would not do any harm to let him in because I was not really doing anything, and his company might be better than no company at all, so decided to relent.

Once inside and seated, he continued with a long recitation of reasons that I should let him into my life. I must admit that at first I was very sceptical, but the truth was that I did not like being alone or feeling lonely. I knew that he was not my ideal mate even though he had features that so many girls would go crazy for, but on the other hand what did I have to lose?

CHAPTER 4

To Have and To Hold

After a short courting period, the inevitable marriage proposal and acceptance followed with the precondition that he would fly to Jamaica and personally ask my parents for their blessings. Within nine months we were married, and Marius was living with me in my apartment, bossing me around, and physically abusing me.

My life had changed dramatically, and so had my demeanour and personality. I worked as a senior official in a local housing authority in the east end of London. I managed a team of staff in the housing department, and we concentrated solely on collecting rents that had fallen into arrears by people who were occupying council housing stock. I was well versed in representing my employers in court, conducting employment interviews for new recruits, holding meetings, doing performance appraisals, setting targets for my staff, writing reports, and other relevant duties. However, nobody would ever have believed the transformation I underwent every night when I arrived home and morphed into a frightened and helpless quivering heap, lacking self-esteem and hope.

The abuse was intense and consistent and it turned me into a shell of my former confident and assertive self. I can remember doing the hour-and-a-half drive home one evening and just sitting in my car outside the house looking up at the lights, which were turned on in the apartment. I must have sat there for over an hour just dreading to go in. I sat outside in my almost-new but freezing Ford Escort car. It was red in colour and my pride and joy, and I had even given her the name—Ruby. I spent hours polishing and cleaning her on weekends, which when I think about, was probably another excuse not actually be inside the apartment. I sat alone watching the white mist of my breath in front of me with my mind whirling around and around wondering what would happen that night. Would it be a slap, or would he just curse me? He had a knack of uttering the most disgusting profanities while demeaning me and telling me how ugly, fat, and useless he thought I was. As I sat in the car, the warm tears flowed, dried up, and flowed again down my frozen cheeks. The abuse was never ending, and my life was totally miserable.

I clearly and distinctly remember coming home one evening and finding him sitting on a chair at the kitchen table. I had worked late that day and had had to battle my way through the traffic from the other side of London. He was just sitting there in the kitchen still in his outdoor coat looking very upset. After making a quick but experienced assessment of the situation, I decided keep out of his way. The sink was full of dishes and I was feeling very hungry so I immediately started to wash up. There was a cut crystal glass on the kitchen table, which I asked him to pass to me so that I could wash it. The glass was part of a set that had been a wedding gift from my team of staff at work, together with a large fish tank. The gifts had special sentimental value for me because the fish tank and all of the other wedding gifts had been stolen from my apartment whilst we were away on honeymoon, and the crystal glasses were the only gifts that we had left after the burglary.

I turned towards him holding out my hand for the glass and watched him as he angrily swiped the glass from the table, smashing it to the floor. I was absolutely horrified and stood there by the sink completely in shock. I knew that it would be unwise to say anything, so I turned back towards the sink and continued washing the rest of the dishes without saying a word. What followed was a familiar tirade of verbal abuse that I was determined would not escalate into a physical altercation. I proceeded to cook dinner only for myself as he had been shouting words to the effect that he was self-sufficient and didn't need a woman to cook or wash dishes for him. After cooking and plating my meal, I decided to eat in my bedroom where I could be in peace.

I carried my food into bedroom and locked the door. Before I could settle in, he began shouting and banging on the door. "I'll break it down!" he threatened. "I've got a hammer!" Then he demanded food. He continued to yell and beat on the door with the hammer until I couldn't stand it any longer. I was so scared I decided to call the police. Luckily for me, the police station was literally only around the corner from my apartment.

In a very short space of time, the police telephoned me back to say that they were outside the front door. I hesitated for a while and then very nervously opened the bedroom door and brushed past Marius. I noticed that the hammer still in his hand as I ran down the stairs to let the police in. There were six of them on my doorstep—four men and two women—and because I had told the dispatcher on the phone that Marius was threatening me with a hammer, they came all psyched up.

The women officer calmed me down and kept me downstairs whilst the male police officers charged up the stairs, immediately restraining Marius as he continued to shout and threaten me. My neighbour, Carol, came out and was very distraught. She told the police that she had heard everything and that the shouting and banging upstairs were commonplace. Carol and the policewomen both urged Carol's daughter, Karina, to go back inside as they noticed that she was also becoming quite upset. By this time, Marius was behaving so badly that the police actually threatened to arrest him. I was completely shocked that he could not even control himself in their presence! Ultimately the police left that night after merely cautioning him because I refused to give my permission to have him arrested. The abuse continued for the next twelve years.

Marius was born in 1960 in the Eastern Caribbean island of Saint Lucia. During the first three years of our marriage we visited the island on several occasions. At the end of a long and particularly relaxing holiday, we arrived at the international airport in Vieux Fort and I asked myself, Why am I going home?' I reasoned with myself that my marriage might be better if we lived in Saint Lucia. I thought that maybe if I could conceive and have a baby life would be better. There was also the fact that I'd had a dream when I was a teenager, seeing myself actually living in the Caribbean. It never actually took much to convince Marius that maybe things would work better for us if we actually lived in Saint Lucia rather than just visiting all of the time, so within a year we had packed up all of our belongings and were living in our own little wooden house in the family compound without our own indoor plumbing or electricity. I soon came to realize that the grass always seems greener on the other side, but it is probably easier to stay on one's own side of the garden even if it looks parched, especially when you have your own family and friends who can lend you a watering hose now and again!

CHAPTER 5

The Seasons of Life

My daughter was four years old when the incident at the church in Castries happened. She had been blessed with two beautiful, deep dimples—one on each cheek. Hope was a gift from God, and I was only able to have her after experiencing two miscarriages, and after enduring five turbulent years of marriage. I can recall the pain of a childless marriage and the heart-wrenching tears that I cried to God beseeching him for a child. I can also remember walking through the city of Castries and staring at what seemed like a never-ending parade of woman who seemed to be blooming and pregnant.

The pregnancy was extremely difficult and resulted in my hospitalisation for two weeks after I found out that I was expecting a child. The nausea was so severe that I was on a self-imposed diet of mint tea, Jacobs Cream Crackers, and Campbell's chicken noodle soup. I dared not eat after midday because the heartburn was extremely severe and I didn't want to suffer with a scourging by fire for the rest of the day. The smell of everything seemed to be magnified one hundred times, and as soon as the wafts came to my nose, I would go a-hurling. There was a lovely mature and heavily laden Julie mango tree close to our house, and the fruits were all rosy and juicy and ripe for the picking. Unfortunately the smell caused extreme bouts of vomiting. The smell of mangoes, body lotion, perfume, and even the smell of cooking led to such severe vomiting that the ejection of even blood and bile were commonplace. After I complained of the awful smell of the mangoes, Marius proceeded to chop the whole tree down to a mere stump. I often wondered afterwards if it would not have been more prudent for him to have just pruned back all of the branches ready for the next season!

I ended up in the French island of Martinique for medical treatment for three weeks, as the doctors in Saint Lucia could not seem to find out what was wrong with me. To my dismay, the doctors in the French island concluded after many tests—all at great expense—that this was my lot, and that I had to go through it as there was nothing clinically wrong with me apart from the fact that I was having a difficult pregnancy. We ended up flying back to London when I was six months pregnant. I spent most of the last three months of my pregnancy in the maternity ward under the supervision of various ob-gyn doctors. Some of the expectant mothers were on the medical ward for the count as there are many complications associated with childbirth. I met Marcia and Felicity there, and we spent many days and nights laughing, crying, sharing stories, and sympathizing with each other as we tried to brave our way through the final weeks of our respective pregnancies.

During my stay in the hospital, I had plenty of time to reflect on my pathetic marriage. I was suffering psychologically from the continued verbal and physical abuse, and I was worried that the stress might have an effect on the baby. At times Marius acted as if he was a raging mad man. On one occasion, when I was about four months pregnant, I had done some tidying up around the house and he became very irritated because he could not find his shaving kit. By that time, I was feeling tired and decided to sit down in the living room and watch some TV. I must admit that when he asked me for his shaving equipment, I may have been a little dismissive by telling him to go and look on the dresser in the bedroom. I probably did not even look up at him when he was speaking to me. He soon came back to report that he still could not find it. I repeated my earlier statement and continued to watch the movie, which was by now in full swing. Suddenly, I felt three heavy blows raining down on my head in quick succession. The blows were so severe that I fell to the ground. While I was down, he proceeded to kick me in the stomach.

On another occasion he told me that the child that I was carrying was not his and that he would have to see the baby when it was born before he could be sure. I really find it hard to think of any greater insult a husband can give to his faithful wife than to tell her that the unborn child that she is carrying does not belong to him. I can remember looking at him with complete and utter disgust after the birth of the baby as he appeared at my bedside in the hospital beaming and stating that he had gone straight to the newborn baby nursery and picked out his daughter from amongst all the other babies. He knew she was his, he told me, because she looked just like him.

~~~

My father died four years later in February 2001 from prostate cancer, diabetes, and resultant kidney failure. I loved my dad very deeply because he was a caring, loving man and was always good to me. I was the youngest of my parents' eight living children, and it felt as if the whole world collapsed on top of my head when he died. I wondered if I was the only one who felt sad, lonely, and empty, as I cried night after night by myself as everyone else in the house lay asleep in bed. I wept bitterly as I remembered my dear father. I could not come to terms with his death, and I mourned my loss long and hard. The deterioration in his health had progressed quickly after he was diagnosed with cancer, and on one of my trips to Jamaica, I noticed the signs of senility setting in. Dad became extremely forgetful and also could no longer hold himself when he needed to go to the bathroom. This was indeed a great problem as he refused to wear the incontinence diapers that were provided for him. This resulted in a strong smell of urine on most of the chairs in the house and on his bed.

The illness had really taken its hold by the time I went to Jamaica to celebrate his seventy-third birthday, but I wanted to make a fuss over him anyway because I wanted to remind him how much I loved him. It was a lovely afternoon, and we had a cake and sparkling non-alcoholic white grape wine and lots of other fun goodies to eat. He seemed to have added a little weight to his meagre frame since the last time I had seen him a few months earlier. Dad laughed and joked and ate, and for a moment it seemed like the good old days as he showed his 'plate'—a reference that he made to his dentures. When I returned to Saint Lucia, I called him frequently just to encourage him and to find out how he was doing. On one occasion I spent quite some time with him on the phone making observations of some of the horrible mistakes that he had made during his later years. I suddenly felt led to ask him to repeat a prayer asking for forgiveness from the Lord, which he did whilst crying uncontrollably so many miles away. Shortly after that call, I was informed that dad had been admitted to the hospital again for surgery, something that he really did not want to go through. He really hated the hospital, and I was shocked to receive a phone call one day from my brother Donald stating that our father had gone missing from the ward. It wasn't until another two days that he was found on the road about thirty miles from the hospital in Kingston. He was dazed and had dried blood all over his body from dog bites and other cuts and bruises. He had been roaming around the streets all that time looking for his home. The phone call that I had been dreading came about three weeks later, and we immediately flew back to Jamaica to start the funeral arrangements.

What made things even worse for me was that, before I could get over mourning the loss of my dad, my mother became ill. A few people I knew informed me that her second stroke was not abnormal given the circumstances; it is not unusual for the surviving spouse to die soon after his or her partner passes away. My parents had been married for over forty years, and like any other couple that had been together for that length of time, they had been inseparable. It was really funny listening to them talk—one of them would start a sentence, and the other one would finish it. Usually my dad would finish my mother's sentences, and at times she took great umbrage to this, which would make him chuckle with laughter and show his huge smile and badly fitting dentures.

I have fond memories of my childhood, and I knew that my parents loved me deeply. I remember my dad as an extremely hard-working man who weathered all climates to bring home the bacon. He worked in a factory making parts for aircraft in a small town called Wembley in North West London. I lived in a three-bedroom terraced house with my parents and my three elder brothers whom I hated because of their wicked and merciless maltreatment of me. Donald, my second eldest brother, used to derive great pleasure by capturing dragon flies or 'daddy long legs' which were flying spider like insects. He would then proceed to deftly dismember them, sadistically placing the legs across the middle of my pillow, after which he'd send me to go and look and see what was on my bed. He would then fall around laughing uncontrollably as I would run around screaming and crying to my parents. My only place of solace in a house with three older brothers was a small nook, which was commonly called the box room because of its size. My mother had a part-time job as a cleaner at the secondary school that I attended. I often felt embarrassed at her having to skivvy after all of the other kids and teachers in the school. I sometimes helped her after school as she performed the menial task of cleaning the toilets and picking up used sanitary towels off the floor. She worked early mornings and in the evenings after all of the children had left for the day. I fiercely hated her having to do that kind of work, but I also understood that it was what helped my parents put food on the table.

I always knew that they were hard-working and dedicated people and that they really tried hard to make ends meet. It was not easy for black immigrants in the UK to survive after they emigrated from the Caribbean in the 1950s, especially because they often had to leave dependant children and elderly parents back home when they went to the land where the streets were supposedly paved with gold. They went so that they could make a better life for themselves and their families back home and in our case they left four children behind in the care of our maternal grandmother. I remember my dad having to walk through three or four feet of snow to get to work in the early 1970s. It was terribly cold, and I watched him from my bedroom window actually lifting his legs up high and then planting his feet down on the ground again, just so that he could walk. There was no bus route to my dad's workplace, but that did not stop him from walking the two and a half miles every day there and back without any complaints. He was just thankful that he could support his family. As a child I looked forward to Friday evenings in particular as I waited for my dad to come home with his usual treat—a big bag of Murray Mints or Pear Drops, which were sweets that he would buy in weighed-out, four-ounce bags. He would give us all a couple of the sweets and then place the bag back in his jacket pocket before he hung the jacket on the back of the door in the bathroom. Of course, I soon conducted my own research into where the rest of the sweets were after eating my allotted share and surreptitiously demolished most if not all of the remainder.

My parents made many sacrifices for us kids in those early days in England, and my mum used to economise wherever she could. I still can't believe how she used to walk a three-mile round trip to the shops pulling her wheeled shopping trolley in order to save a few pennies on bus fare so that she could buy an extra tin or packet of something. The shopping trolley was always really heavy, and she also had to carry extra plastic bags filled to the brim with the week's groceries. My teenaged brothers refused to help her because it was not considered cool to be seen with your mum doing the grocery shopping. I used to help her most of the time, but to be truthful I think that my help was limited as I only went for the liquorice sticks which she bought for me from the Holland and Barratt health food shop in the Wembley Central Square.

When I thought of the loss of my dad, and the love that my mother had always shown me, I fell into despair. I cried all day and all night at the possibility of losing my mother as well. I did not seem to be coming to terms with my loss, and rather seemed to be becoming increasingly sad with each passing day. My mother agreed with my request to return to my house in the UK for a six-month visit so that she could recouperate. It was at that point that I left my job at the bank in Saint Lucia as a loans recovery officer and returned to my family home in London. So we left for the UK in the summer of 2000 to care for my sick mother who had suffered her second stroke within a month of my father's death. I never expected to be in such emotional turmoil, but everything hit me a lot harder than I had anticipated. I was determined to take care of my mum as I was not prepared to let her go just because dad was no longer around.

CHAPTER 6

Once a Man, Twice a Child

Everyone was really excited about Mum's arrival, and we had arranged for special assistance from the airline for her all the way from Norman Manley Airport in Jamaica to London Gatwick. She came through the customs hall walking stick in hand, but riding in an electric car driven by a Virgin Atlantic steward. As soon as I saw her face as she emerged from the arrivals hall, my heart skipped a beat and tears of joy began to stream down my face.

I couldn't wait to get her home as we chatted all of the forty-six kilometres or so from the airport to my house in the town of Wembley. Everything was spick and span and ready for her. Marius and I had moved out of the master bedroom and fixed it up with a brand-new queen-sized bed, flowers, and a painting . . . everything was looking really pretty. After Mum eagerly settled in, she sat down and ate her lovingly prepared steamed red snapper and okra, carrots, sweet potatoes, and fresh garden salad. She was a diabetic as well as being a two-time stroke survivor, so I had made a special effort to shop for lots of fresh fruit and vegetables and assorted types of fish because I was determined that she was going to get well. Mum loved being back in England and longed for her favourite foods, some of which were not as readily available in Jamaica as she would have liked, or just too expensive for her to be able to buy with any frequency. One of her greatest pleasures when she had lived in England prior to emigrating to Jamaica had been to spend hours going around all of the shops buying a little here and a little there. It was great fun for her to see all of her friends and acquaintances along the way and to stop and chat endlessly with them about all sorts of things. That was in the good old days when she was strong and healthy and walking . . . that was then.

Everything was great. Marius was behaving and even helping out with Mum and our daughter Hope from time to time. I felt that we were becoming a real family. I was now able to ensure that Mum was taken care of properly and that she had everything she wanted so that she could start to recover from Dad's passing.

One of the first things I did was to ask the social services department for assistance in the form of bereavement counselling. A lady came around to the house once a week and spoke to Mum about the loss of my dad. I sat in on a couple of these sessions and noticed that Mum never really talked about Dad at all. I found this a little odd and asked the bereavement counsellor why she was not steering the sessions around talking about Dad and how my mother felt about his loss. The counsellor responded that discussions during the sessions could go anywhere my mum wanted them to and that she was only there to listen. I remember talking to Mum one day and becoming quite disturbed when she told me she wouldn't mind getting married again if someone asked her. I thought this was a rather incredible statement for

37

a sixty-three-year-old woman in a wheelchair to make and wondered if she had forgotten Dad already. I thought it would be much more appropriate for her to concentrate on getting better and living out her remaining years quietly.

Social services were actually quite fantastic and provided and installed a chairlift to take Mum up and down the stairs. Thursday was social club day, and the bus would arrive in the morning and take her off to a local community centre where she would meet and socialise with other seniors. It was great for her, and I was very pleased that she could get out of the house and have lunch and play games as well as share stories with her newly found friends. The physiotherapist came around to the house twice a week to retrain her to walk and to use her right arm properly. He tried to get her to make herself a cup of tea or to do light washing up in the kitchen and make simple meals by opening a can of soup for example.

Mum seemed to go along with all of this, but after some time it became pretty obvious that she preferred not to put herself through the rehabilitation process, and she even seemed to become quite resentful. Mum soon got tired of the healthy fish dinners I had been preparing and wanted things like fried bacon and ginger beer or malt instead. Normally the bacon might not have seemed much of a problem, but it was a totally unacceptable development to Marius who refused to allow pork to be stored in the fridge or cooked in any of the pans that were being used to cook his food. Marius had a religious conviction about pork. He felt it was unclean because of a story in the Bible in which Jesus cast the demons out of a man and sent them into pigs. He strongly believed that pig meat should neither be eaten nor handled. He had similar views on mackerel, herring, and all shellfish.

The purchase and cooking of pork at home caused many heated arguments between my mother and Marius, during which they exchanged numerous unkind words. After a few weeks of looking after Mum, giving her insulin injections, cooking, shopping, and cleaning, I began to feel the strain. Hope was going to preschool every day, and Marius was at work as a labourer with a local construction company. In effect then, I was at home with Mum every day and at her beck and call. At one point I felt as though I was suffocating in the house. Nothing I did seemed to be enough for her or was done properly any more. She would moan about this, or moan about that—the tea was never hot enough, or she wanted to watch a certain TV program when everyone wanted to watch something else, or one of a hundred other things.

I remember speaking to my friend Cecelia about the strain that I had begun to feel with looking after Mum and not being able to have a break away. I explained that I felt as though I needed some time away from home, because of the pressure that she was putting on me mentally and emotionally. It was on one of those days of pouring my heart out to her that she asked me if I wanted a job at the offices where she worked. I looked at her with incredulity and asked her if she was serious. She assured me that, if I wanted the job, it was mine.

I was so excited about working again, especially as some of my former colleagues were still working in the same office after eighteen years. My job was mostly administration, which entailed writing reports all day and interviewing families who may have fraudulently applied for assistance from local government. There were only three of us in my section, and we all became very close. We were all women around the same age, and we were all very professional and dedicated to the job. We turned over a lot of work between us, and we were well respected by the other departments that we worked with. We were like the fraud squad, weeding out fraudulent aid applications and saving the council hundreds of thousands of pounds in payments. The job was great, and I really enjoyed working with so many different people. Unfortunately, though, at this stage I had started smoking because of all of the stress with my home life. It was an old habit I had picked up briefly when I was in my mid twenties, and I started to practice it again pretending to myself that it helped me to cope better.

I had arranged with my supervisor at first that I would go into to work early and then have a longer-than-usual lunch break so that I could go home and prepare Mum's lunch. I would rush home and make her something light, and then rush back to work. However, Mum complained about the lunch not being sufficient for her and not nutritious enough. I then arranged to have social services deliver 'meals on wheels' to her at lunchtime. They even installed an intercom system so that she could let the driver in at the door without having to go downstairs to open it. The food was great and consisted of a lunch and a dessert all wrapped up in foil trays and still piping hot. This all seemed great, especially as a home help caregiver would also come around in the mornings to help her to bathe and comb her hair. I now had some time away from the house, and Mum could still be cared for, not to mention the fact that I was now able to supplement the household income.

Hope was approaching primary school age, and we had been trying for another baby for the past three years. Nothing seemed to be working, so we had just started to attend appointments at the local hospital to investigate why I couldn't get pregnant. It was just about six weeks into the start of my new job that the doctor confirmed that I had conceived, and I remember that my knees buckled underneath me as I left the doctor's office after hearing the news. I felt elated and scared all at the same time. I sat in the car for about half an hour shaking uncontrollably, unable to start the engine because of the news.

I told Marius about the baby that evening and he seemed quite pleased; however, I wasn't quite sure how I was going to tell Mum. I delayed telling her for a couple of days because I was not sure of how she would react as she had become quite belligerent, constantly nagging and demanding. As soon as I came home from work each evening I would have to attend to her and the rest of the family right away, and I was not coping very well at all. I asked Marius to help with the dinner sometimes, but Mum refused to eat his food saying that it was not cooked or presented properly. She wanted me to cook and serve her dinner, give her a dose of insulin, and then bathe and change her into her nightwear. She also liked a hot cup of tea and a snack before bed, and I found it increasingly difficult to keep smiling while also caring for my daughter and a difficult husband. At first I tried to manage, but soon I was starting to feel quite tired and miserable.

I decided to see if I could evoke my mother's wonderful mothering character, which I had grown to love over the course of my life. She was in bed one evening, and I climbed in next to her feeling quite nervous about how I was going to broach the subject. At first we spoke generally about this and that and nothing at all in particular, while all the time I was trying to pluck up enough courage. Finally I just said it: 'Mum, I went to the doctor the other day. I'm pregnant.' There was a long pause while she gave me a really disgusted and questioning look. 'Again?' she finally said. I asked her what she meant as I had only one child. This prompted her to give me a good tongue-lashing. 'Why couldn't you have used protection instead of letting yourself get pregnant for that lazy chicken man!' Mum reduced me to tears by telling me that that I should have an abortion and that God would forgive me afterwards. I reminded her that she'd had eight children, none of whom she aborted, and that I was a married woman living in my own house with my own husband. I could see nothing wrong with me having a second child, but she was adamant that I should 'throw away my belly.' I left her bedroom and wept bitterly.

The coming months were almost unbearable, and I was so sick that I was forced to spend more time at home than I did at work. I felt both embarrassed and guilty when I told my supervisor and colleague about my pregnancy so soon after starting the job. The timing of the whole thing really seemed to be way off. They were really understanding at work though, and were always telling me to slow down and rest, go for a walk to get some fresh air, or just stay at home if I needed to. I was reduced to sitting at my desk with a plastic cup covered with tissues that I used throughout the day as a makeshift sputum cup because my salivary glands were in overdrive. I was forced to walk around with the cup or empty soft drink tin at the supermarket, on the bus, at church, or anywhere else for that matter. The morning sickness lasted all day and all night, and I vomited persistently throughout the whole gestational period—the same unfortunate feature of my first pregnancy.

The side effect of all of this was that I was feeling emotionally and physically drained. I could hardly make it out of bed most mornings, and eating dry toast to stop the nausea didn't help at all. Life wasn't made any easier by Mum as I still had to see to her needs whether I felt equal to the challenge or not. Actually I never got a scrap of sympathy from Mum; she was as demanding and implacable as ever. By this time, she was refusing to eat the food that was still being delivered by the meals on wheels service, and I had to prepare her meals myself. I felt this was nothing less than torture. I had no energy left, and this was not helped by the fact that the little that I did eat refused to stay down. At one point, I called the doctor out for a home visit, because I was feeling very poorly indeed. I explained to him how I was feeling, and he recommended that I be admitted to hospital for rest and recuperation. I refused to go, explaining that I had responsibilities to my family and that it just was not possible to leave home. The doctor warned me that I needed to undergo tests, and unless I was admitted to hospital, my situation could become much worse. After much deliberation, we decided that I would go and have the tests done as an outpatient and then return home to my family.

My daughter was oblivious of what was happening to me apart from the fact that I had a baby in my tummy and that I was sick all the time. The truth was that I did not have much of a bump at all, and even the people who worked in the same general office with me were unaware of my medical condition as there was nothing visible at all even after seven months. In fact, when I passed out invitations to my leaving party, people asked me where my next job was going to be! I told them that I wasn't going to another job, but was leaving to have a baby. Most people were startled as they hadn't realized that I was even pregnant.

In reality I would have liked to stay on the job longer, but this was not realistic considering the state of my health and the time that I had already taken on sick leave. I looked drawn and haggard, and I was not sleeping well at all. I also had to contend with Mum's failing memory and her not being able to find her money most of the time, which she then accused me of stealing.

I overheard her complaining to the Home Helper about it one day, which left me feeling completely gutted. Mum was receiving disability allowance from the state, some of which came in quite handy for buying her food and treats. It was my responsibility to go to the post office every fortnight and cash in her allowance and bring it to her. She would then give me money to assist with expenses around the house and buy her groceries, but all of a sudden she could never find where she'd put her savings. I remember cleaning her room really nicely one day. I rearranged the room and put on fresh bed linen to make her happy. This turned out to be a big mistake. She became very angry and accused both Marius and me of using the cleaning of the room as an excuse to rob her. I am still unsure if this was the beginning of senility or if she was just being downright malicious.

One Thursday I asked her if she wanted me to help her to get ready for her social club and she got really upset. She replied that I was trying to push her out of the house and that she had every right to stay in it for as long as she wanted every day. She said that I was trying to get rid of her and that she did not want to go to the club any more. At that point I became very annoyed and told her that she was going to go and that I would get her ready. I began to dress her quite roughly, and as I pulled the comb through her hair, she began to cry. She didn't stop complaining during the whole episode, but rather kept going on and on and on. At one point, I actually covered her mouth with my hand and she bit me, and it was all that I could do to restrain myself from actually retaliating.

I finally agreed to go into hospital for a three-week rest, and my eldest sister was forced to take Mum in. During the six months that Mum had stayed with me, my sister had come to see her only twice, and my eldest brother who was living in Wales would not agree to help as he said that he did not have the room to keep her, although he did come and see her from time to time. My other siblings were overseas and therefore unable to assist with mum so I was forced to cope more or less on my own. I know that my siblings all loved Mum, but I suppose that they just could not commit themselves to the amount of time and effort that were needed to undertake the task of taking care of her. In retrospect, I can understand that now. Caring for the elderly and infirm is no small feat, and those who are in the medical or care giving professions must be the most amazing people ever and have a special gift of compassion which can come from only God himself.

CHAPTER 7

Strange Happenings

It was not long after I was discharged from my hospital rest and had returned home that Mum started complaining about seeing things. She would become quite irritated and say that she could see black-winged objects flying in front of her. She said that there were lots of them in the room and that they were all around her. At times she would use her hands to brush them away from her face, and at other times she would shout at them and tell them to leave her alone. Mum said that they were flying demons that had come to torment her, but I simply dismissed all of that as just more of her drama.

I can remember that when I was a child growing up in the UK, Mum and Dad would make references from time to time to *duppies*—a Caribbean word for ghosts or evil spirits. For us, duppies and 'rolling calves' which is an evil spirited animal were particularly scary, and our parents would tell us frightening stories about some of the things that they had either seen or heard about when they were growing up in Jamaica. Neither my siblings nor I took these stories seriously and just passed them all off as figments of their imagination.

As an adult, my opinions never changed much either, as I certainly did not believe in duppies or ghosts—or anything else of that nature. I realized that Mum had started to change her Christian perception during the early 1980s, when I was just a teenager, after becoming friends with a gentleman by the name of Mr Antrobus. When he invited Mum to attend some 'church' meetings, she accepted and went along with him probably twice a week. I was never taken along to those meetings, and I did not know where the meetings were actually being held or what they did there either. That in itself was quite strange when I think of it, as I used to go almost everywhere with Mum when I was younger, not willing to let her out of my sight for a moment. I always felt that I was her protector or guardian and was quite happy to tag along whether it was day or night.

I did see various pieces of literature and books start appearing around the house, though, and they were all connected to the Church of Scientology. I really had no idea what the church or the books were about and I never asked. I am sure that as a teenager, I must have had much more pressing matters to think about, and as long as she was happy, that's all that would have mattered! I also think that, because the titles of the books had the word *church* in them, I must have thought that they were legitimate because I was brought up to believe that the Church was a place where Christians were and where all that was good abounded.

Mum and Dad emigrated to Jamaica from England in the spring of 1987 right after dad had celebrated his sixty-fifth birthday. During my frequent visits to their new home, I sometimes noticed an old lady visiting at the house whom I knew to be called Sister Ellington.

I later found out that it was this woman who introduced Mum and Dad to another alternative 'church' that taught its members how they could help themselves in life by keeping their enemies away and how to supposedly protect themselves from evil spirits. I remember asking Mum about this once and also about the meaning of even more new books I had found accumulating in the house. I flipped through some of them one day, and I noticed all sorts of strange-looking symbols and characters. Mum said that the books were educational and explained the powers of the human body and how humans could leave their physical body behind and travel from place to place. In short, Mum and Dad had been lured and had fallen into a dark trap. They soon began to go and visit various obeah men to help them with whatever problems they perceived they had.

In the Caribbean, witchcraft is also often referred to as obeah or juju, beliefs that stem from ancient African origins. The wide-spread practice of these dark arts is recognised as a religion today, but it is a religion that it is not compatible with Christianity at all. However, a combination of superstition, fear, and inquisitiveness seems to lead so many people to its perilous shores—and to their own demise.

I suppose my parent's problems must have really started in earnest when they bought a piece of land to build their house on in the busy town of Old Harbour in the parish of St. Catherine in Jamaica. They paid cash for the property and built a large, three-bedroom, two-bathroom bungalow and fenced it in on a plot of about 17,000 square feet. After they built the house, some neighbours moved in next door and after a short time, they began to insist that my parents were encroaching on their land. The dispute lasted for years between the parties, and each side sought help from the underworld as well as the formal legal system.

I remember Mum complaining about the neighbours one day as she noticed an array of red plastic bags hanging on the neighbours clothesline in their garden. Mum became very upset, promising that their evil would not work against her and that they could not prevent her from prospering. I surmised by Mums reaction to the red plastic bags that they must have had a malevolent significance. On another occasion, both Marius and I were on holiday staying at my parent's house. Very late one night my parents woke us up and asked us to go outside of the house and wait. We were made to stand outside in our nightclothes for at least an hour while two women went inside and started to burn incense and chant prayers. Mum and Dad and my brother Donald had left the house hours earlier to go and pick up these women in a taxi and bring them to the house. I later found out that the women lived about twenty miles away, and my parents had paid for the entire round trip for them, as well as whatever remuneration they required for the service they provided.

When we were finally allowed back in the house, the air was still thick with the smell of the incense. It wasn't long after that, whilst cleaning one day, that I noticed all sorts of strange markings—pentagrams and other shapes—under the rugs on the floors of the bedrooms. Some family Friends also informed me years later, that there were also weird markings on the roof. I asked Mum at the time what all of these things were for, and she offhandedly replied that they were put there for 'protection'. I guess it was a case of fighting fire with fire, and my parents had forgotten everything the Bible had taught them for years:

'For the weapons of our warfare are not carnal, but mighty through God to the pulling down of strongholds' (2 Corinthians 10:4, KJV).

Similarly, when I was on another holiday visit to my parents' home in Jamaica, I suddenly became quite irritated upon seeing a stack of curious 'arts' books. I decided to tear them all up and burn them. I took all that I could find far out into the backyard and set them alight. I must say that I felt very proud of myself as I thought that all of that stuff was a load of rubbish anyway and that my parents were certainly better off without it. A few days after my book burning, Mum started going around the house asking for them. I admitted to her that I had gotten rid of them; needless to say, she was very upset indeed with me.

One night when Marius and I were sound asleep in the room next to my parents' room, suddenly my dad burst through the door shouting and demanding that the duppies should get out of the house. We were obviously very startled and wondered what was happening, but dad kept going on and on saying that they should get out and that he knew what they had come for and he would not let them succeed! After some time, he calmed down a bit, and we were allowed to go back to sleep. The next morning I asked Mum what the problem had been the night before and she replied that the duppies had come to kill Daddy but he had seen them before they could succeed, and he had chased them away. I really did not know what to make of these goings on, and I chose not to dwell on them because they were all too far beyond my understanding.

After much heartache, confrontation, and adjournments at court, it was finally decided that my parents had in fact unwittingly encroached on their neighbours' land. Apparently the realtor who sold the land had not identified the boundary pegs correctly and caused them to believe that the plot of land that they had purchased was actually much bigger than it really was. This was a matter that could have been easily resolved years before by simply engaging a land surveyor to measure the land according to the survey plan. All in all, it was quite an unfortunate incident, and it probably contributed to my second eldest brother losing his physical life, and my parents losing their spiritual lives.

While many people in the Caribbean still cling to their beliefs in the dark arts, we, the English generation, just dismissed all of this talk of duppies, rolling calves, and obeah as nothing more than superstitious mumbo jumbo. We laughed at our parents when they started to go on about things that went bump in the night or that they had heard and seen—or rather *thought* that they had heard or seen. I suppose that more than half of the time neither my siblings nor I placed any credence in any of these stories. Now I realize that the real truth is that some form obeah is probably practiced in every country that you can think of. Obeah is witchcraft, and there are different names for it depending on the country or culture that it is practiced in. There are various well-established variations on the theme in England, North and South America, China, India, Africa, the Caribbean, and everywhere else in between. The Bible says that 'men loved darkness rather than light, because their deeds were evil' (John 3:19, KJV). But the Bible also warns that 'the wages of sin is death' (Romans 6:23, KJV), and so if you practice witchcraft you are a servant of the devil and will not partake of the kingdom of heaven. It is noteworthy to remember that having your palms read, following your horoscope, or using a Ouija board are all occult activities.

CHAPTER 8

End of a Long Journey

Six months had now passed and Mum's time in England was up. This was a big relief to me. I had collected lots of her favourite goodies and gifts for various members of the family and packed them securely in her bags. The baggage allowance was forty-four kilos in those days, so she made sure that she had lots of frozen bacon, apples, and Aero mint chocolate bars. As a matter of fact, her luggage was seriously overweight, but the baggage check-in assistant was really sympathetic to this old lady in a wheelchair who I explained was emigrating to her homeland. I couldn't believe that she was actually going back home.

I was feeling very queasy on the morning of her departure, but I was determined to ensure I went to the airport myself and saw to it that she actually left the country. I wanted to pinch myself to make sure that I was not dreaming as she started to disappear out of sight. I stood at the barrier alone, with my eyes transfixed to the back of her wheelchair as the attendant pushed her through. I stood there for what must have been no less than twenty minutes just watching the sign that said 'passengers only beyond this point'. I stood there as long as I could, wanting to make sure that she was really gone. I tried to pull myself together and then realized that I was hungry, so I decided to go and get some breakfast in one of the airport fast-food restaurants. Whilst I was eating, I noticed that I was trembling because I was actually totally famished. I wolfed down the toasted chicken sandwich and hot chocolate and sat for a long while trying to regain my composure, reassuring myself that Mum was on a plane bound for Jamaica.

I had to catch three buses home from London's Heathrow Airport, and although the November air was crisp, I welcomed the fact that I could be on my own without having to worry about anything or anyone for just as long as the journey lasted. I chose to sit at the very front of the upper deck of a big, red, double-decker bus, as they were known, so I could look through the wide expanse of window for a good view of the streets in London and people going about their daily business. A warm rush of peace and happiness came over me, but I still refused to believe that she was actually gone. In fact, I told myself that I could only be sure if I went home and proved it for myself, and that thought caused me to start to panic. I somehow convinced myself that she would still be in her room when I got home. I started shaking again, and all of a sudden an uncontrollable urge to throw up came over me. Before I knew it, my clothes, the floor, and the seat where I was sitting were all in a mess. I wretched and wretched until there was nothing left. I couldn't believe that it had happened again, and on the bus of all places! I acknowledged to myself that it would have been worse if there had been anyone else around, but I alone occupied the whole of the top deck. I tried to clean myself up as best as I could, and I changed seats. When I reached my destination, I disembarked.

A strong feeling of trepidation came upon me when I pushed the key into the lock of my very own front door. Slowly I closed the door firmly behind me and walked resolutely straight up to her room. Although she was not there, I felt her presence. It was almost tangible, and it scared me. I looked through the rest of the house and I confirmed that it was empty. Slowly it began to dawn on me that Mum was not there anymore. I could not help but just sit there in the living room—not even bothering to take off my coat—and crying uncontrollably.

I had assumed that Marius and I would move back into the main bedroom when she left, but I couldn't. The most I could do was to strip the bed and discard all of the stuff that she had not carried with her. I flung open all of the bay windows and moved the bed into another position near to them. Over the next few days, I sprayed air freshener and perfumed carpet cleaner and bought scented air freshener that was meant to be plugged into the electrical outlet for all day freshness. Yet still, it felt as though Mum was in the room. After a while, I realized that I was overreacting and probably being quite silly about the whole thing. Mum was long gone, and I was not about to let her to continue to make me feel like a hostage in my own house. I suggested to Marius that we repaint the main bedroom and move back into it ourselves, which we accomplished quite quickly.

At first everything seemed fine, but then I started to have some very strange and vivid dreams. One night in particular, I dreamt that I was on the operating table in the hospital and there was a team of doctors around me working frantically to save my life. It was as if I was looking down on myself as they did all that they could to save my life. I woke up feeling very disturbed indeed, and when I explained the dream to

Marius, he brushed it off saying that it was just a dream. There were many other quite vivid dreams to follow, which left me feeling scared, even to the point that I feared going to sleep because of them.

During one of my antenatal visits, the doctor explained to me that I had the choice of opting for a normal delivery or a caesarean section. The hospital that was providing my antenatal care always gave mothers a choice if they had previously had a caesarean. My daughter had been delivered by caesarean due to the fact that my waters had been broken for seventy-two hours and my body had refused to go into labour naturally. As I thought this over, I remembered the dream that I'd had where I viewed myself on an operating table in a hospital emergency room. I could only imagine that this was a warning to me and that I should avoid having another caesarean at all costs. I informed the doctor that I wanted to try for a normal delivery this time. Everything was arranged nicely, and my bump was getting bigger and bigger with each passing week. From time to time I would feel some sharp kicks under my ribs in the chest area. These jabs would always make me jump, and I hated the uncomfortable feeling when the baby was turning inside my tummy. It must have been a peculiar sight to see me lying down on my side with three pillows supporting my huge belly, but it was the only way that I could rest comfortably.

As the weeks went by and the expected date of delivery grew closer and closer, I decided to buy one or two things for the baby. I was trying to overcome my superstition that it is unlucky to buy anything new until a baby is actually born. The people at the antenatal clinic were always giving expecting mothers samples of creams and diapers and talcum powders, and I had quite a little collection of these items at home. I had also avoided buying any clothes because the hospital that I was attending refused to tell mothers the sex of their child before it was born. I remember going for an ultrasound one day and asking what sex the baby was, whereupon it was explained to me that it was hospital policy not to give out that information because some mothers from some Asian communities aborted the foetus if it was not male. I also suppose another one of the reasons that I had failed to buy anything for the baby was the memory of two past miscarriages. I didn't want to get my hopes up too high unless I was sure that the baby was actually going to arrive.

I spent most of my days at home watching the shopping and holiday channels after the short drive to drop Hope off to preschool. It was there that she played and learned and mingled with kids of her own age, and it eased my conscience a bit as I had started to feel guilty about her being an only child. For the entire period of gestation, I believed that I was having a girl because of the shape of the head and face in the ultrasound image. I even compared the ultrasound scan images of the new baby with the images of Hope when she was still in the womb, and they looked identical. The truth be told, I would have been quite happy with whatever the Good Lord gave me, and was very grateful to have come this far.

I whiled away the days dreaming of far-away warm and exotic places that I saw on the Holiday Channel. As I watched the shopping channels, I found myself buying a bread-making machine and a set of knives that were so sharp that the manufacturers offered a lifetime guarantee and many other items some of which I didn't really need. Sometimes I would take a stroll up to the town centre with my coat flung wide open as I drank an ice-cold can of something whilst not even minding that it was the dead of winter and bitterly cold outside. My time was more or less my own during those days except for the keeping of periodic hospital appointments and collecting my daughter from preschool in the afternoons. When she got home, we would sit together and enjoy her favourite programmes, *Bear in the Big Blue House*, *The Flintstones*, and the *Golden Girls*. We would play games, and I would comb her hair and read her stories before bed.

By this time, I no longer enjoyed going to church on Sabbath, as I found the pews to be very hard and uncomfortable. When I did go, I would spend most of the time during services shifting from side to side, but not being able to find a comfortable position. The baby also had a habit of moving around quite a lot. With this discomfort, coupled with the heartburn, I just thought it better to stay at home during the closing weeks of the pregnancy. The brethren came to visit, though, and I looked forward to the encouraging phone calls that I received from the pastor and his wife and also some old friends. For a while I could enjoy being the centre of attention rather than have to focus on anyone or anything else.

The drama began early one cold April morning when the house was still asleep. The pain was so harsh that it violently shook me from my slumber. I checked the time. It was about six in the morning, but it was still very dark outside. The heating was programmed to come on at half past six, so the house was still very cold, and I could feel the chill even when I was still under the blankets. I quickly collected my thoughts and eased myself up from my sleeping position onto one elbow and lay there for a minute. Suddenly another seriously sharp, shooting pain ripped through my body. I screamed. This prompted Marius to come into my bedroom to ask me what was wrong. I had opted to move back into the spare room, which we had occupied when Mum was staying with us, as I needed more space at night to stretch out and turn. I told Marius that the baby was coming and that he should call the hospital and let them know. I continued to roll myself out of the bed and felt thankful that my bags were already packed. All we would have to do was get ourselves ready and then go off to the hospital. When we dropped Hope off at preschool, I explained to her that the next time she saw me, the baby would be out of my tummy and that she would be a big sister. She seemed very excited, but also not a little nervous about the whole thing. She kissed and hugged me and walked away slowly and deliberately to her class. She was dressed in a little, white, furry coat with big red spots on it and a matching hat and gloves that made her look so adorable, especially with the deep dimples on either side of her face. The snow outfit was finished off with red Wellington boots that protected her little legs from the severe winter weather.

I let out periodic screams in the car whilst Marius drove me to the hospital, which was approximately eight kilometres away from where we lived. I had to be brought into the maternity ward by wheelchair, and I remember waiting in the reception area while the nurses found my notes. At that point the pangs and the accompanying screams were coming every five minutes or so, and the other expectant mothers glanced at me uneasily as they observed what their own fate might well be soon. I was taken to the labour ward and checked by a midwife, but the sack containing the amniotic fluid had not yet broken. Soon, she came back into the room and explained that she had to break the sack and release the fluid so that the baby could be born. I assumed that from the point that she did this, everything would be over quite quickly; however, after over twelve hours, my cervix had only dilated three centimetres. Unfortunately, I was there for many more hours, and the pains seemed to get more severe as the time dragged by.

I thought that the contractions were quite extraordinarily severe and also close together. I gripped the side of the bed and let out almighty screams. At one point, I asked Marius to come and hold my hand. He had been sitting on the other side of the room looking very upset and disgusted with me. He had never even had the presence of mind to ask the nurses for any pain relief on my behalf. I was so engulfed in pain that I never thought of asking until eleven o'clock that night when it dawned on me that I could have had something to help me and I was given an injection to help relieve the pain. It was soon after that that I realized that I could no longer see anything except reds and yellows and blues. All the time I was able to hear and sense my surroundings, but everything was a blur of different colours, and I could not see anything plainly.

Later in the night, I heard a nurse come in, and I realized that she had come to stand close to my bed. She was there for a few moments when I heard her saying that there was something that was not right. I heard her say, 'She's crashing! She's crashing!' Hurried footsteps then went through the swing doors whilst I continued to scream. A few moments later, I heard many more voices. There were men and women talking over me. All of a sudden, the back of the bed on which I was lying was folded down flat, I was being pushed out of the room, and people were running with me down the hall to the operating theatre. Something deep down inside me made me realize that something was very wrong indeed, and I knew that the terrible dream that I'd had a couple of months before was coming to pass.

Since I realized that I probably would not survive this experience, and that I was completely helpless, I decided to commit myself into the hands of the Lord. I began to recite out loud the Psalm 23, Psalm 91, and also Psalm 121 over and over again. The doctors were by this time in a frenzy and I felt them, inserting tubes and placing monitors on my chest and inserting a drip feed into my wrist all at the same time. I could hear many concerned voices all at once, and all of this was taking place while the pain continued to rip through my body. 'Don't stop praying,' I heard a man say as I felt a cold liquid running through the veins in my left arm. In my heart I knew that I could never stop praying even as I quickly and completely floated away into another world.

CHAPTER 9

Precious Jewels

My eyes opened heavily, and for a moment I looked around the recovery room. At first I thought I was alone, but when I turned my head to the left I saw the cradle next to my bed. My instinct was to move across the bed and see what was inside, but it was impossible. I felt as if I weighed about ten tons, and I was unable to move. I was experiencing a combination of disorientation, grogginess, and numbness all at the same time. After a few minutes, I decided to call out, which alerted a nurse that I was awake.

She soon appeared at my bedside smiling very sweetly whilst asking me how I was feeling. I told her that I felt sore, and she tried to comfort me by explaining that this was to be expected as I had just been through a major operation. I continued to lie still on the bed for a moment before the nurse asked me if I wanted to see the baby. I was feeling so drugged up and sleepy that I hadn't even asked if the baby was well. I continued to lie back on the bed whilst the nurse put the baby into my arms, and I proceeded to look into the most beautiful eyes imaginable. The face was the face of a tiny angel, small and smooth and soft. I stayed like that just looking at the baby, and after some moments I asked if it was a girl. The nurse totally shocked me by replying that I had given birth to a bouncing baby boy! *How odd*, I thought, because I had been totally convinced the whole time that the baby was a girl.

I lay there beaming down at my son, unable to rock him or comfort him as I felt too weak, only managing to smile at him adoringly whilst asking how much he weighed. I took in every detail of my son's features—his full head of straight, black hair; his large, dark-brown eyes; the long curly eyelashes; and his incredibly hairy earlobes. His skin was flawless, and his cheeks and lips were tinged with a pinkish hue. I watched as his entire hand curled around my index finger, showing tiny white knuckles. It was Good Friday morning, and I knew that I was holding a tiny baby and a huge miracle, but soon I realized that I felt very sleepy and I was unable to keep myself awake. The last thing I heard was the nurse's reply as she answered six pounds, thirteen ounces. I felt myself drifting off to sleep again as she gently took the baby from my arms.

I drifted in and out of consciousness for some time. I was only somewhat aware that visitors were trying to communicate with me, but I was not in a position talk back to them with any degree of sustained coherence. The following day I was feeling much more alert, and I was moved onto the general ward with the other mothers and their babies. The nurse came in to see me during the afternoon and told me that I had to try to get out of bed and start walking around. For a moment I looked at her incredulously and then informed her that I was still in an incredible amount of pain. I was soon given two small pills that shortly put me back to sleep and completely eased the pain for some hours afterwards. When the pain relief wore off, I would press on the call buzzer that was connected to my bed and wait for the nurse to come around again. Finally, she refused to give me any more, explaining that they were addictive and that she would ask the doctor to give me something else. *How disappointing*, I thought, as those little pills seemed to knock me straight out and kill the excruciating pain that I was feeling in my lower abdomen after the caesarean section that I had just had. We had not chosen a name for the new baby, partly because we were expecting a girl and partly because we wanted the child to be born first. My dear friend Cecelia visited me in the hospital and requested that the baby's first names should be Malachi Caleb, but I decided to switch the names around and call my son Caleb Malachi instead. Marius had no opinion—as usual—on the name of the baby, so the matter was easily settled.

~ ~ ~

It was grey looking outside, but there were strong rays of sunshine coming through the hospital ward window. I decided to pick Caleb out of his cot and give him a little breast milk as he hadn't been feeding very well. I carefully placed my son on my breast, but he refused to wake up. At times I would shake him very gently, and his eyes would open very heavily and then quickly close again. There seemed to be very little that I could do to arouse his interest. I persisted with this throughout the day but then also noticed that his skin was looking a little yellow and that the whites of his beautiful eyes were also taking on a strange yellowish hue. I decided to report this to the nurse, who in turn called a paediatrician to examine him. The doctor assured me that the baby looked fine to him and that it was not unusual for newborn babies to sleep a lot and not to feed well at first.

However, I was not convinced with this response. My maternal instinct kicked in, and I decided to hold the baby on my tummy toward the window where strong rays of sunlight were shining through. The following day was the day that we were due to be discharged from the hospital. When the doctor came to visit us during his rounds, he asked how I was feeling and how the baby was. Again I explained that the baby was not feeding and was sleeping all of the time. I further explained that the baby's eyes were turning yellow and that his skin was pale. This doctor confirmed that there was nothing wrong with the child and that he was perfectly healthy and I could take him home that day.

It was at this point that I insisted on seeing a senior doctor because I was not happy with the condition of my baby. After I waited a further four hours, the doctor finally appeared at my bedside. He asked me to again explain my concerns, which I did in quite an exasperated tone. I stated that I was not prepared to leave the hospital until my baby had been properly checked over. The doctor then ordered some tests to be done, which included taking a sample of blood from Caleb's tiny foot. After I waited another three hours or so, the senior doctor returned to tell me that the baby had a severe case of jaundice and that he had to be admitted immediately to the intensive care unit for treatment! Before I knew what was happening, a nurse whisked Caleb away from my arms, placed him in a portable cradle, and wheeled him off somewhere far out of my sight.

Another nurse told me that I was free to go home; I could visit the baby at the hospital whenever I wanted, however I refused to go. I told them I wasn't prepared to leave my baby there in the hospital alone. My immediate reaction was to burst into tears whilst exclaiming that I had known—better than the experts—that something had been wrong all along. Nobody had listened to me!

After some time had passed, I asked for directions to the intensive care unit—or ICU as it was called. It seemed as though I had to walk miles to get there as it was situated well away from the maternity ward on the other side of the hospital building. I walked along long corridors and past many closed doors to different wards that housed people with all kinds of ailments. I entered the elevator and pressed the button to a lower floor. The elevator came to a jolting stop, and I grimaced as I felt a severe pain rip through my lower abdomen near the site of the incision. I was wearing warm bedroom slippers that were furry and comfortable, but my pace was slow and deliberate as I dragged my feet heavily in search of my son. It seemed to take me ages to arrive to the spot where my baby now lay. The sister in charge escorted me to the place where he slept, and when I saw him, I completely froze with shock.

There were tubes coming out of my little boy's nostrils. Another tube, which was attached to a drip, went into his little arm. There were little adhesive circles pasted to his chest. Monitors alongside the incubator where my baby slept clicked and flashed with readings and lights. All of this looked far too overwhelming for my tiny son to cope with. He seemed so fragile and pale as he lay sleeping on the miniature mattress, which was neatly and playfully covered with a teddy bear motif. There was no pillow though; his little head rested to one side as he lay on his back.

The Sister-In Charge compassionately helped me to sit down as I burst uncontrollably into tears again. I think I was almost on the verge of fainting or screaming or hitting somebody or something, but I was not sure what. I felt angry, frustrated, sad, betrayed, and I suppose grateful all at the same time. Although all of this had happened, the doctors and nurses reassured me that they had found the problem in the nick of time and that the baby was receiving the best medical care. The doctor told me that drugs were being administered to my son intravenously and that they were giving him a specific time period to respond. He explained that Caleb's bilirubin levels where critically high, and if there was no improvement shortly, they would have to administer a full blood transfusion.

I stayed for hours by his bedside singing and praying and crying. At one point I asked the Sister if I could hold him and see if he would nurse, and she agreed. I sat down in a very comfortable chair as she took Caleb out of the incubator and handed him to me. I immediately tried to breast feed him, and although he opened his tiny mouth, again he did not seem particularly interested. I continued to hold him in my arms for about half an hour, but the Sister told me that he needed to go back into the incubator. After some time, I left the ICU and returned to the maternity ward where I was served dinner, but the last thing on my mind was food. How could I eat knowing that my baby was lying so far away from me hooked up on wires and tubes? After a short rest, I decided to go back and see my son, but this time I was not permitted to hold him in my arms. Sister explained that the monitors had indicated that that the bilirubin levels in Caleb's blood had risen even more during the period that he was out of the incubator.

We stayed in the hospital for a week in total and were discharged when the doctor gave us the all clear after he examined Caleb and gave him a clean bill of health. We returned to our home to find it cold and dirty. There was little or no food, and I had no choice but to call for a delivery from a fast food restaurant. My appetite had returned to normal; in fact, I was eating like a horse as breast-feeding made me feel hungry all of the time. Hope was ecstatic about being a big sister, and she laughed and played with the baby and sang to him at every opportunity. I was now placing my focus on the children and also on getting myself well again. I had left the hospital with strict instructions about not doing any bending or stretching, lifting, or heavy housework. I tried as best I could to heed the instructions of the hospital staff and also of the nurses who came to check on us at home, but I still had to take care of things including the cooking and looking after the welfare of the children.

It was still very cold outside, and the snow was on the ground. The hospital had given me a few days' supply of medication for the pain, and the pills had just run out that morning. At around ten o'clock that morning, Marius left the house with a refill prescription in hand for my painkillers. The round trip to and from the drugstore should not have taken more than an hour, but he failed to return. I tried calling his mobile phone only to find that he had switched it off. Hours passed by, and I was reeling in pain again as I had long since taken the last pill. At around five in the evening, I decided to call around to see if anyone knew of his whereabouts. Nobody was able to tell me that they had seen him. At ten o'clock at night I decided to call the police and all of the hospitals in the area in case there had been an incident somewhere and he had been admitted.

Again, neither the police nor the hospitals had seen a man fitting his description, and by then I felt totally confused. At midnight the house was quiet, as the children were fast asleep. As I looked through the bedroom window, I noticed that the snow was crisp on the ground. The streetlights spread an orange tinge on the mounds that were piled by the side of the road. The street was quiet except for the occasional car that zoomed past without obstruction. I craned my neck looking left and right, up and down the street listening for the familiar sound of the white Mazda 323 we had purchased for a mere £500 almost a year before. The car was great and always started the first time we turned the key in the ignition, even in inclement weather. It had become an essential for us especially with the school runs and hospital visits. Now I stood by my bedroom window looking out at the lonely road wondering where it had taken the father of my two children

It wasn't until late into the night that the familiar sound of the engine woke me from a very broken sleep. I momentarily lay in the bed in order to collect my thoughts, and then slowly eased myself up. I positioned myself at the bedroom window and noticed that the car was now parked outside at the kerb in front of the house. I immediately turned and slowly walked down the stairs to the front door. I stopped about four feet away and watched a figure slowly emerging in front of the double glazed door. Soon I heard the sound of the key turning. Finally a very bedraggled and exhausted-looking Marius stood before me. He just closed the door and stood there. I said nothing and waited for an explanation as to why it had taken him all day and half the night to return home from a trip that should have taken him less than an hour.

'Hello, Hannah,' was all he could muster up as he brushed past me to go up the stairs. I turned around and watched him as he climbed the complete flight and turned into the hallway that led to the bedrooms. I thought that I must be dreaming as I stood there incredulous at the gall of the man. I was so angry that I began to tremble as I followed behind him. I entered the bedroom with all of my guns blazing. 'Where have you been until this ungodly hour?' I asked.

He then proceeded to explain that he had met an old school friend from Saint Lucia who had invited him home for a drink and chat for old times' sake. He had lost track of the time. I asked him why he hadn't called to let me know where he was, which prompted him to further explain that he had forgotten the house phone number. He said that, after having a few drinks, he had fallen asleep on the couch and had only woken up a short while ago. Still trembling with anger, I reminded him that I had been in the house all day with no medication and two small children. I also told him that I had been worried and had called his relatives and the police and the hospitals looking for him. When he heard this, he flew into a rage, shouting that he was a grown man and entitled to go out wherever he wanted and to come back whenever he wanted and that I should make sure that I never again tried to track him down or call anyone to ask about his whereabouts. At this, I turned on my heel to answer the call of a now awakened newborn baby, vowing to myself never to discuss the incident with him again.

Whilst we were in London, Marius encouraged me to sell the flat that I had purchased years before. He explained to me that it made little point in owning two properties and not having enough money to live comfortably. He said that it was far better to keep our family home and sell the flat so that we could use the money to finish off the house where we lived in Saint Lucia. He said that we could extend the property and add solar hot water and our own electricity and water supply instead of sharing with our neighbours. For years, we had been sharing a utility supply with his mother and his brother's family who lived in two separate houses very close by. Each month, a member of the family brought the bills to me, and I had to pay them. When I asked Marius and his brother why it was my sole responsibility to pay the bills that their family had incurred, they subjected me to a string of profanities.

I must admit that I could see both the merits and demerits of his argument about selling the flat, especially the part about having more of my own funds, as I never liked to live hand to mouth. The flat had been an investment, and as such I had never really wanted to part with it. I thought it was quite an achievement to have been paying my own mortgage and to be driving my own car by the age of twenty-one, and I really wanted to hold on to the property if I could. However, Marius did not have a job in Saint Lucia, and we had planned to leave England when the baby was three months old. I couldn't bear the thought of scraping around again, especially with the additional expense of a newborn. I finally capitulated and put the flat on the market. We soon found a buyer who was willing to pay me almost double what I had paid for it originally so many years ago.

All during the time that the property was on the market, Marius kept on telephoning the realtor to ask about the progress of the sale. I was unaware of this fact until one day when I had to call their office. When I asked the agent for the date of the exchange of contracts with the purchaser, which is really the point of no return between the two parties, he informed me that my husband had already called that day and received the information. This actually annoyed me to no end, as I felt that the details of the sale of *my* property should have been kept confidential, as I had not given them permission to divulge it to a third party. I sharply rebuked the realtor and asked him to note that they were to give out no further information without my permission.

Once he found out that the property was actually sold, Marius turned on the pressure even more. His behaviour worsened, and he started demanding that I give him his share of the money as he needed to buy things to put in a container for shipping back to Saint Lucia. He stated that he needed money to buy equipment so that he could start his own decorating business. I refused to give him any cash despite the intense pressure. He finally goaded me into buying a concrete mixer, double length ladders, a pressure washer, power tools, a mountain bike, clothes, shoes, and all sorts of other things. He was very angry with me because I refused to tell him how much I had actually received for the flat. He cursed me heavily and continuously.

I had real money of my own now, and money meant power and possibly freedom for the kids and me. I was now the mother of two children. They were my responsibility, and I knew that they could count only on me for their survival. Their biological father, to put it mildly, in my opinion was less than a responsible person, and I was not about to let him blow away our newfound opportunity.

CHAPTER 10

The Darker Side

Within two weeks of our return to Saint Lucia, when Caleb was about four months old, I booked airline tickets to Jamaica for myself and the children so that they could see their grandmother. My brother Donald met us at the airport, and all of the family were really happy to see us. My mother's house was clean and looked quite nice, with everything in its place when we arrived. There were three double bedrooms and two bathrooms. The master bedroom and bathroom were en suite, and this area was occupied by my brother, his girlfriend, and his two small children. Mum had the room to the front of the house, and I stayed in the room to the back of the house, which I had long since adopted as my own. The house was over seven hundred meters in size and included a very large carport and balcony area. There was also a large room off the kitchen that doubled as a storeroom and a bedroom depending on the need at the time. However, the kitchen was not a place to visit at night simply because of the hoards of tiny cockroaches that infested it. You would need only to go in and switch on the lights to see scores of them scattering as they ran for cover. It was just one of the unsavoury things that I hated about that house, but no amount of fumigation or insecticide could ease the problem. Another thing I disliked was the foul stench that came from a culvert that ran alongside the house. When it was blocked, strong and foul odours emanated from it, and I found it difficult to stay in the house or sleep at night.

Mum nicknamed the baby Short Legs and tried to hold him as best she could, but she was still suffering from a broken left arm, which she had sustained after a recent fall. Everybody adored the children, but Caleb was the centre of attention. He was actually very quiet and well behaved and only made a fuss when he was hungry. My brother's girlfriend at the time took pleasure in looking after him if I needed to go into the town to run errands. We put large pillows on either side of him to stop him from moving around too much on the bed, but he was quite happy to be left without having to be held all the time. I loved to go out into Old Harbour town centre, which was located in the parish of St. Catherine, and look around the fruit and vegetable market and pick up supplies. On the way home, I would treat myself to some lovely beef patties or the most wonderful-tasting jerk chicken and festivals which were made from flour, baking powder, cornmeal, salt and sugar and formed into a sausage shape and then deep fried. I would always make a bee line to a particular a street-side vendor close to a very large upright clock in the middle of a very busy thoroughfare. Until I returned home, my son would just lie quietly on the bed smiling and cooing playfully waiting patiently to be breast-fed.

Mum seemed to have mellowed quite a lot as far as the baby was concerned. She had probably resigned herself to the fact that he had arrived and there was nothing she could do about it. She had become a complete invalid by this time, and had to be bathed and taken to the toilet or helped to her chair, which was located in the veranda next to the carport. The garden was quite extensive to the front of the house, and she would spend hours every day sitting there looking out over the long driveway, which led to the very busy main road. I would sit there with her, and she would complain about and ask me questions about the 'lazy chicken man' I had married. Mum had never really liked Marius, especially since the trip I made to Jamaica in 1998 when I told her that he was physically abusing me. I didn't actually tell my dad, but instead chose to confide in her explaining that he had given me a black eye one morning.

Before Caleb was born, when Hope was really small and we were still living in Saint Lucia, Marius was working as a painting contractor. He employed a crew of about five men. He had delegated to me the task of making up the workers' wages every Friday according to their daily rate and the number of days that they actually worked. I was not paid for this unwanted chore. One Friday evening he came home stating that one of his workers had complained that his pay had been shorted. I asked him if that was true, and he stated that he didn't know. I then proceeded to ask for the worker's name, the daily rate, and days in question. When I checked, these were all in order and corresponded to the wages that I had paid. Marius then went on to explain further that the worker was demanding that he be paid double for working on a holiday, which prompted me to enquire whether Marius had agreed with the workers that he was paying a special rate on holidays. Marius had made no such agreement with the workers, and so I explained that he should be clear and precise about the daily rate when he hired people for work. I emphasised that he should inform the men before employing them that he did not pay overtime rates, and every day was a standard day. A discussion that I thought should be obvious and straightforward turned into a huge row that lasted all night.

Marius said that I was the one who got him into trouble with his workers and that everything was my fault. He said that the men threatened to beat him up for their money, and it was something that I had planned from the start. He ranted on and on. Even when I was getting ready for work early the next morning, he followed me into the bathroom where I was taking a shower. It was about six o'clock, and he was standing just in front of the shower curtain saying that I was useless and couldn't even add up simple wages for his staff without making a mistake. He was cursing and shouting and really carrying on and not prepared to let the matter drop at all even though I pointed out that I had done only what he had asked. At the time, I had been employed as a loan recovery officer at a local bank for just about two weeks and I had to be at my desk at about seven forty-five in the morning. I definitely did not want to be late for work; however, I finally decided to defend myself by telling him that he was the one who didn't know what he was doing. I asked him why he didn't make up the wage envelopes himself rather than giving them to me all of the time. I told him that he was an uneducated and foolish pig and that he should get out of the bathroom and leave me alone to get ready for work.

In an instant, Marius ripped the shower curtain to one side and flung an almighty punch to the right side of my face. I slowly sunk to the tiled floor hitting my head on the tiled shower wall as I fell. I saw only greens, blues, reds, and oranges before my eyes. I remember that Hope, who was also in the bathroom at the time, started to cry, but I was unable to comfort her. Although I never passed out, I couldn't see anything. Marius eventually ended up wrapping a towel around me and bringing me up to my room. All the while he was exclaiming that I had made him do it because I had been rude and disrespectful to him. Whilst lying on the bed, and clutching the side of my face, I could hear him saying that he loved me and that he was sorry, but I had been the cause of the fight. I am not sure whether Mum and Dad ever forgave him for that, and Mum certainly never forgot about the incident. When she spoke about him, there was always a certain graininess in her voice, and her face would contort noticeably. Although I could empathize with her, for some reason I still was not comfortable with her open criticism of him and her sharp words even though they were very well placed.

That morning I ended up calling into work sick and then sending in a sick note for a week's leave. The right side of my face had dropped visibly, and the skin had turned a purplish black. My eye was swollen shut, and the lid had overlapped. I had a headache for about three days and lay in bed crying endlessly about what my fate would be with this man. I didn't think I could go on living this way for much longer. I needed time to think and was not sure of what to do, but one thing I knew was that I was very unhappy with my life.

I returned to the bank after my sick leave had ended but soon realized that people had noticed that I had a black eye. I really tried my best to cover it up with liquid foundation makeup and blusher, but my efforts made it look more ridiculous than anything, and people could still see my facial bruises. A close colleague of mine came to me and informed me that people were talking about me. They did not believe that I had fallen as I claimed because I had no scratches on my arms or legs, but only one big bruise on my face. I decided to brave the inevitable embarrassment and to come clean about the whole thing. I told her what the actual problem was. She recommended that I speak to my line manager who was actually the assistant branch manager, and I decided to comply with her recommendation. It was actually a great relief to be able to speak to someone and tell him about the dark secret that I had been keeping to myself for so many years. He was surprisingly sympathetic to my plight and advised that I take a further two weeks off work to sort myself out. He asked me if there was anywhere I could go away from my home to think and refocus. The only place of relative safety that I could think of was my parents' home. He suggested that I spend time with my parents and formulate a plan of action, as my situation had become life threatening.

After returning home to Saint Lucia from my trip to my parents' home in Jamaica, I moved into a one-bedroom rented house about ten miles away from where we had been living. Marius soon found me, though, much to my dismay and came knocking on the door. Saint Lucia is a very small island with a population of only 160,000 or so people. Everyone knows everyone, and his sister had spotted my vehicle which was parked on the road outside the house that I was renting, and reported it to him. He quickly came to reclaim both me and his daughter, who was only about eighteen months old at the time. I refused to move back home, but the inevitable apologies, begging, and pleading went on for eight months until I decided that it might actually be safe to return home. He explained that I should not waste my money paying rent on an apartment when I could live in my own house free of charge. He promised that I didn't ever have to worry about him hitting me again as he would report himself to the police station if he even so much as sucked his teeth at me or look at me sideways. I reasoned that it was preferable for our daughter to grow up with her father, and that if he was going to behave, then I should give him another chance, and so I returned to the house.

~ ~ ~

Four years later I sat with Mum on her balcony. Whilst I plaited her completely grey hair, she colourfully recounted the reasons she hated Marius. 'He is a worthless and lazy chicken man, and he doesn't mean you and the children any good. You have let him walk all over you and eat everything you have worked for, and now you have another baby on top of it. I never liked that man; you could see from the start that he was lazy and useless. He might have a nice face and look good, but it's the character of the person that matters.' What she was saying was true, but I felt that, for the time being at least, I was in between a rock and a hard place.

That night, I put the children to bed after applying some Vicks VapoRub to the soles of their feet and chests because they had just started sniffling. I lay down on the bed next to them. I was feeling very tired after a full day cleaning and washing and cooking for everyone in the house, and I soon drifted off to sleep. I then started having the most vivid and terrifying dreams one after the other. I saw a strange black thing looking like a cross between an animal and a man in silhouette. This 'thing' dragged me off the bed and onto the floor. I saw myself literally kicking and screaming and punching this thing as it tried to get me out of the way so that it could get to the children. I woke up in a cold sweat and felt exhausted as if I had really put up a fight for my life. The strangest thing, though, was that I had the same dream for three nights in a row, but I never mentioned it to anyone.

On the fourth night I decided to ask for assistance from my brother to place the mattress from my bed on the floor of my mother's bedroom. I explained that we wanted to be nearer to Mum, but the truth was I was no longer comfortable sleeping in that room. During the day, I kept the room door firmly closed and went in there only when I needed to get something from my suitcase. By now I had felt a very strong and tangible presence in the room; I felt as if something in there was watching me. I sensed that it was big and dominating and evil in nature, and I was afraid.

For the first night, Mum didn't say anything about us sleeping on the floor in her room, but on the second night she asked me why I was there with the children and not in my room. I explained to her that the smell of the culvert at the side of the house was too overpowering for me and that I preferred to sleep in her room. After a long pause she answered me. 'You think I don't know why you are sleeping in here? What have you seen? They are very out of order to trouble you, and they should leave you alone.' I just looked at her in amazement but never uttered a single word. That night I lay beside the children on the mattress and tried to sleep. Again I felt a tangible evil presence in the room, and I felt convinced that this presence was after my children. The whole night passed as I lay there refusing to sleep. My arms were stretched across the children in a protective hold whilst I prayed and prayed in earnest to God for our care and protection.

The next day I decided to confide in my brother Donald and tell him what had been going on. To my surprise, he didn't seem at all taken back by what I was saying. He said that he too had experienced several strange encounters in the past. He described that on one occasion he was sleeping and that he was awakened when he felt something ice cold on his arm. When he opened his eyes, he saw a huge figure made up of white dots but in the form of a human. He said that when he saw the thing, he screamed out loud and the thing ran away. He could literally hear the thud, thud, thud of its footsteps as it ran down the side of the house by the culvert. I told Donald that I was sure that all of this stuff must have been happening because of the witchcraft activities that Mum and Dad had engaged in. I also told him that I did not feel comfortable staying in the house any longer. I had a few more days to go until the end of my vacation, and those days were particularly difficult for me because of the continuous dreams, which I suppose could have been called visions because they were so real. Although my home in Saint Lucia was not ideal, at least I could sleep at night in peace—or so I thought.

CHAPTER 11

Cold Hands, Cold Heart

Marius became very distant towards me and even more belligerent, treating me with absolute disgust most of the time. He was hardly ever at home, and when he was, I wished that he would leave again because we always fought. For all intents and purposes, I was all alone in Saint Lucia with two small children and no family of my own, although I did have two dear friends in whom I sometimes confided.

Marius would leave the house for a week at a time, and when he did come back it was as if the whole house was on edge. He would open the door to the house and his heavy footsteps would make the floorboards shake. As he entered, he would throw his keys across my hand-carved, six-seat Italian dining table, which he knew that I prized. It was a deliberate act designed to irritate me as I had begged him time and time before not to do it as it only succeeded in scratching the highly polished wood on its surface. By now, I was resigned not to respond to him and rather chose to ignore his many outbursts. I would choose to sing or put my favourite CDs on to play selections of Hillsong praise and worship music, or one of Donnie McLurkin's albums.

The latest of his pet peeves was that he wanted me to buy him a new pickup truck so that he could use it to transport his ladders and workers to and from work sites. The truck would cost about $EC70, 000 after the application of a duty free concession, but the bank would not give him a loan because he did not have steady work. He ranted and raved daily about needing a truck and that I had all of the money tied up under my skirt. He told me that he was going to get it from me. He cursed my mother, my dead father, and me continually. The filth of his language was extreme and never ending. He told me all kinds of hurtful things, saying that I was big and fat and ugly and that no man would ever want me. He said that he was doing me a favour by staying with me, and that I was useless. He continued to abuse me verbally but never touched me physically, but at a point I almost wished that he would hit me instead of cursing me nonstop, because, whilst the bruises would clear in a few days, the mental notes that I had made of all the insults would probably never go away.

It was when I realized that I could not take any more that I finally relented. However, rather than pay for the vehicle outright, I agreed to stand as guarantor for a loan at the bank. I told him that I would place my money on a fixed deposit at the bank as surety for him, but that he would be responsible for making his own monthly repayments. He reluctantly agreed to this and within a few days he was driving around in a brand-new, olive-green pickup truck. Boy did he worship that truck. He washed and polished it constantly, getting his nephews and cousins to clean and shine it even when there was a speck of dust on it. One day I remarked to myself that he never helped with the housework or the children and didn't show even a quarter of the interest in his family as he did that truck.

Once he bought the truck, he would be gone for days at a time with no word. He had found a new lease of life thanks to the truck, and normally came home in the wee small hours of the morning. On one particular night I lay awake on the bed with the two children unable to sleep. The house was silent and the loud music from the surrounding family and neighbours had long been switched off. I was soothed by the deep but gentle breaths of the children as they lay next to me. Suddenly I heard the doorknob turning, and I quickly fixed my gaze on it. The wooden house had been constructed in two phases with a concrete structure below that contained the bathroom, kitchen, and dining room, and a wooden structure above that consisted of two bedrooms, a living room, and a bathroom. The bedrooms were at the back, and the living room was at the front. Between them was a door that was lockable and operable only if you were on the other side where the bedrooms and bathroom was situated . . . I was used to Marius coming in at all hours of the night and banging on it whilst in a drunken stupor, asking to be let in.

On this particular occasion, I waited for the customary bangs and shouts but none came. I continued to look at the door, and the knob turned again. Then there was silence. I was then shocked to watch before my very eyes a door that could not be opened from the outside, opening wide with an invisible hand. I lay still, completely shocked, somehow still expecting to see Marius come in, but there was no one there that I could see, and I soon came to grips with the scene that had unfolded before my very eyes.

I jumped off the bed, rushed to the entrance of my bedroom door, and blocked it. I shouted in a loud and authoritative voice: 'You devils in hell that have come to my house to torment me and my family, I come against you with the blood of Jesus Christ of Nazareth, and I arrest you in your tracks now! I plunge the sword of the spirit though your heart, and I twist it in deep and warn you that no weapon that is formed against me shall prosper! You, agent of hell, hear me now. I am calling forth a tsunami, an earthquake, and the Holy Ghost fire from heaven to burn and destroy and crush you right now. I know who I am in Christ Jesus, who is my elder brother, and I am using the power that was given to me by my father in heaven, the same *dunami*spower or delegated authority—that Jesus gave to his apostles to bind and cast you out of this house! I am calling forth the sheriffs from heaven to send you back to the abyss right now. I am risen with Christ in heavenly places, and I have the power to trample you under my feet, so get out of my house now!' I immediately started to pray. 'Father in heaven, Mighty Man In Battle, Jehovah Nissi and Conquering Lion of Judah, I am presenting myself before you now in the name of your son, Jesus Christ, and I am complaining to you that my home has been violated by the evil ones. Please send your warring angels to these workers of iniquity now, ready for battle with their swords drawn. Dear Lord, send sufficient in number and sufficient in strength to annihilate them and cleanse this house now. It is written that my body is the temple of the living God, and even as you dwell inside my heart, so I dwell inside this house. Daddy, do your work now and persue, overtake and destroy them right now! In Jesus name I pray. Amen.'

Even I was not prepared for what happened next. I opened a side door of the house which had a curtain hung in front of it for privacy. As soon as the door was opened, the curtain started flapping wildly, and I sensed that whatever was in my house was now being forcefully ejected. I stood aside for a while, just watching as the curtain grew still again. There was no storm outside, and the night was perfectly still. I concluded that this indeed had been the hand of my God at work just as I had requested, and I felt at peace and was contented enough to go back to bed and fall soundly asleep with my children.

There were other strange happenings as well. Marius came home in the early hours of one Sunday morning as drunk as a skunk. I opened the door for him so that he could go to bed, and I went back to bed with the children. At first he went to his room, but he soon came into the room where I lay with the children and started to pull me off the bed. I kicked and pushed him, but he was much stronger than I. I got hold of my Bible and shook it at him telling him to leave me alone, but he refused. I reminded him that he was supposed to know the word of God about committing fornication with different women—and about drinking alcohol and smoking marijuana. I told him that he had turned his back on God, and reminded him that the wages of sin was death. When he heard what I was saying, he knocked the Bible out of my hand straight across the room and onto the floor. He pulled me off the bed holding one of my legs and I fell heavily to the floor. He then dragged me across the hallway into his bedroom and hoisted me up throwing me violently onto his bed. He raped me, all the time telling me that I had no right to refuse because I was still his wife.

Later on that night and in the very early hours of the morning, he came into the room where I lay. He was whimpering and brushing his hand aggressively in front of his face. 'Leave me alone, I'm so sorry, just leave me alone!' He kept repeating himself over and over again, and I sat up on the bed watching him with a perplexed but weary look on my face. He was by now waving his arms around and twisting back and forth, obviously trying to knock away something that only he could see. 'Hannah, please help me!' He begged and begged until I eventually asked him what was wrong. 'They are attacking me, and they won't leave me alone.' I asked him who was attacking him and he just replied that the flying things were hurting him, and that I should help him.

I got off the bed and watched the man as he slumped to his knees in a posture of prayer by the foot of my bed. 'You fool,' I said. 'You are not a big man now, are you? You just knocked the word of God out of my hand and raped me, and now you are asking for mercy. There is no repentance in the grave, so repent now, you wicked sinner!' He replied by saying that he wanted to repent, and so I told him that if he was serious, he should repeat the sinner's prayer after me, which he did. Nevertheless, the unseen things were still attacking him, and he was weeping like a baby. I stood over him and watched him curl up into the foetal position with his fists clenched underneath his chin. 'Look at you now,' I taunted. 'What do you see? How is it that only you can see them? What are they doing to you, and what do you think I can do about it?' He was crying even harder now and was rolling around on the floor still knocking away the invisible enemy.

I decided to leave Marius where he was and go into the other room to call Pastor McLorren. Pastor answered the phone at four o'clock in the morning. I apologized for the ridiculous hour and explained what had precipitated the phone call. Pastor said that the young man was under an attack that was orchestrated by the devil and that he had opened doors in his life for that attack by his behaviour earlier. Pastor said that I should agree with him in prayer and then launched in to a long and fervent prayer of rebuke of the hand of the devil over the life of Marius. When he had finished praying, Pastor asked me to go and see what Marius was doing. I did as requested and returned to the phone shortly saying that he was still writhing and brushing things away from his head and body. Pastor resumed the prayers and again asked me to check what Marius was doing. I told the pastor that he had calmed down a bit but was still not normal. Pastor continued the prayers, and I checked Marius again. By this time he was completely still. I thanked the pastor whilst noting that it was almost five o'clock on that Sunday morning.

When I arrived home from church later that morning Marius was sitting on the balcony with a very angry expression on his face. 'Where are you coming from?' he demanded. I answered that I was coming from church. Marius then proceeded to declare that, from that day, I would stop going to that Sunday Catholic Church as it was a false church. He viewed any church that did not hold services on a Saturday as a Catholic church regardless of the real name of the assembly or the denomination, so the Pentecostal church that I was attending fell under that heading. I answered him by saying, 'Oh really?' I continued past him and, as I entered the house, he stood up and continued shouting very angrily saying that if I continued attending the church, then I would have 'no more husband' and that he would not look after anybody's children whilst they went and gave false worship to Sunday gods.

From that day on, I made up my mind that I would no longer attend the Seventh Day Adventist Church as I felt that I could not get many of the answers that I needed from that assembly. I figured that, through all the years that I had been suffering in bondage, no one there had helped me identify the problems that I was experiencing or had offered me any prayers or guidance. I craved knowledge in the ways of God, and I became an avid reader of the word of God, and worshipped and read and received counselling and strong Bible teachings. I needed practical direction on how to be an overcomer and how to be an effective prayer warrior and servant of Christ. Marius was not a real Seventh Day Adventist, and his hypocritical nature was not typical of the behaviour of true followers of the faith. To be honest, he had been backsliding for years, and judging from his behaviour, I figured he had probably never even been 'saved' in the first place. I entered the house but did not bother to reply to his statement. I knew that Marius did not have any power over me anymore, and in my mind I had long ceased believing that in any practical sense there was any substance left in my marriage anyway. I knew that my marriage was over and that I would leave him. The question for all intents and purposes was not *if* but *when*, and I just didn't have the answer to the question at that point in time.

CHAPTER 12

The Final Straw

On one particular afternoon, the phone rang. It was a lady from the bank once again asking for Marius. As usual, I informed her that he was not at home, and she asked me to let him know that she wanted him to attend the bank the next morning at nine o'clock sharp regarding his loan. These calls had been coming regularly since I had stopped making his truck payments, and it was obvious that he was not making them either, but I no longer cared because I was not benefitting from the truck anyway. I remember that on one occasion I asked him if I could take it out for a spin, and he refused, stating that I would probably wreck it because I could not drive. I then reflected that I was actually the person who had taught him how to drive whilst we were living in England. When we returned to Saint Lucia, he had refused to take his driving test legitimately, but rather opted to pay someone in the licensing authority to provide him with a new and valid driver's license. Once he came in that evening, he saw the handwritten message that I had left on the bed in his room. The only thing he asked me was the time that the lady from the bank called, and I informed him that she had called that morning.

I supposed that his financial problems worked themselves out, as the lady from the bank stopped calling and he also seemed a bit happier in himself. I never bothered to ask him anything, because we were really living separate lives although technically we were still living under the same roof. I thought that, as long as he was staying out of my way, all was well, and I had learnt over the years to let sleeping dogs lie.

One morning I decided that I needed to go to town to withdraw some money from my savings so that I could do some grocery shopping and pay some bills. Upon arrival at the bank, I asked the cashier for the amount that I wanted to withdraw and gave her my savings passbook for updating. When she handed the book back to me, I noticed immediately that it reflected a deposit of five thousand dollars cash. I stood for a moment looking at all of the entries and the new balance, which I could not understand. I asked the teller what the credit was for. I informed her that I knew that God was good, but even so, I did not believe that it was he who had put that extra money on my account! The bank teller admitted that she was not sure what the credit represented, but that she would find out for me and have someone call me before the end of the working day.

I can remember that the phone call came at around five in the afternoon. After verifying who she was speaking with, the female caller identified herself as an officer of the bank who was calling to answer my earlier enquiry about the source of the credit on my account. The bank officer then proceeded to inform me that the five thousand dollars that was showing on my savings book was the balance of my fixed deposit that had been broken at the request of my husband in order to pay off his vehicle loan. After a long pause, I asked the lady on the other end of the phone to repeat what she had just said, because at that point I was sure that I must have missed something.

Unfortunately, the lady on the phone provided me with no comfort, but merely clinically repeated her earlier statement, leaving me only then to thank her and replace the receiver on the telephone hook. I stood there just looking at the phone feeling completely miffed. It was at this point that I knew that the straw had broken the camel's back. I sat in the living room and thought about what had just transpired. I realized that things had become totally out of control and that I could no longer stand by and watch Marius destroy me—and the children's future. I just could not believe how callous this man was. What he had done angered me to no end; nevertheless, I prayed about the whole thing and asked God for wisdom in the matter. I purposed in my heart not to say a word to him when he came in, and I managed to get through the evening without event.

The following morning, I took the children to day care and then marched off to the bank with a great resolve to get my money back. That was all the money that I had in the world, and it represented the dwindling balance of the proceeds of the sale of my flat a couple of years earlier. I knew that I had to get the money back, and I was determined to ensure that the bank did exactly that. Upon entering the bank, I waited in line. When it was my turn, I asked to speak with the loans recovery manager. The customer service representative walked away from the main banking hall and disappeared behind a partitioned wall for a few moments. She soon returned and explained that the manager was not at his desk and enquired if I had an appointment. I advised her that I did not have an appointment and that if the loans recovery manager was unavailable, then I wanted to see his manager instead. She asked me the nature of my enquiry, and I explained that I had a complaint about the handling of my account. After a few moments, she ushered me into one of the upstairs offices away from the main banking hall and asked me to be seated whilst I waited to be attended to.

After about five minutes, a gentleman came and sat down behind the desk where I was waiting. He leaned forward and greeted me, shook my hand, and introduced himself as Mr Robertson. He asked how he might be of assistance to me, and I launched into a passionate, detailed explanation of what had transpired on my account. I told him that I wanted the transaction to be reversed.

'You see, Mr Robertson,' I explained, 'I believe that I had a right to be formally notified by the bank that my husband's loan was in arrears. At least then I would have been given the opportunity to speak to him about the matter myself. The bank had no right to just take my entire life savings and pay off someone else's loan without my knowledge or consent. This kind of thing is totally unethical, and I know that there are rules and procedures governing this kind of thing, and in my case I am sure that they have not been adhered to. Let me be straight with you, Mr Robertson. I want the money that was taken from my account to be replaced before the end of the working day—every last penny of it—otherwise I will go to all necessary lengths to have this matter brought into the spotlight.'

The manager asked for the account details, so I handed him my passbook. He then started tapping heavily at his computer keyboard. All the while I sat stiffly and quite pokerfaced in the chair not willing to remove my steely gaze for even one second. It was then that he explained to me that Marius had visited the bank and instructed that his entire vehicle loan be paid off from the proceeds of *my* fixed deposit and that the bank had acquiesced. My voice became very stern as I explained that Marius did not have the power to instruct anyone—not even the bank—on what to do with *my money*. I told him that I found the bank's behaviour to be quite unreasonable and unacceptable in the circumstances. 'I am simply not interested, Mr Robertson, in my husband's problems. Please replace my money!'

The manager stood up and walked away from his desk with some printouts and my savings passbook in hand. He disappeared out of sight whilst I sat and wondered what was going to happen next. I had prayed and asked God for inner strength and wisdom and also for his help in this matter. I took the next few moments to beseech Jehovah-Jireh not to allow my enemies to triumph over me and to help me out of this insufferable situation. I wondered about the fate of my two children and how I had let them down by not protecting them from their father. There is no way that we would be able to survive without any money. We had no immediate relatives whom we could ask for a loan or shelter, and without money, we would surely be destitute in a foreign land. The children were still very small and vulnerable. It would take money to send them to school and provide them with even the basics that we needed. What would I do if the bank did not give me back my money?

Whilst my mind drifted, I was jolted back into reality by the ringing of a nearby telephone. As I refocused, I realized that Mr Robertson had re-emerged and that he was looking very unhappy indeed. He retook his position at his desk and once again started banging at the keyboard muttering loudly to himself. 'I keep telling these people that bad loans are bad loans irrespective of whether they are guaranteed, and that it causes more harm than good in approving them.' Soon the bank manager handed me back my updated passbook. He apologized for all of the obvious inconvenience that I had been caused. I opened the book cautiously and turned to the last page, which contained the most recent entries. There it all was—every penny that had been taken had been credited, and I knew then that I had been given another opportunity to put things right in my life.

I returned home and sat alone in the house on the sofa and tried to think. I knew that if I stayed with Marius, I would end up dead, destitute, or completely mad, but I wasn't sure of what I needed to do. I decided to get a piece of paper and a pen and write down the pros and cons of staying in the house with him, or leaving and finding my own place with my children. Even I was amazed that it only took me about five minutes to come up with four single lines of reasons why I should stay and almost two full sides of A4 paper filled with reasons why I ought to flee for my life with the children. I realized that at least I had options and that I had a means to exercise them.

I believe that I had allowed fear to overwhelm me, and this had prevented me from leaving this abusive domestic relationship years earlier. The stigma of having a failed marriage and also the sheer inability to believe that I could make it on my own had held me captive. My self-esteem was at an all-time low, and the continuous abuse was so debilitating that I believed in his lie that I would never survive. I had to find inner strength, pull myself up by the bootstraps, and face the reality that my marriage was destructive and that I had to leave as soon as I could. Staying in an abusive relationship can destroy the victim and leave long-lasting scars. As I look back on my own story now, I would advise any victim of such abuse to escape and seek the appropriate support as soon as practically possible. Help is available in the community or from friends or family.

CHAPTER 13

A Safe Haven

It wasn't that hard to find a place to live because I was a realtor and had begun to build up a small list of contacts who either wanted to sell, rent, or buy property. I decided to stop working in Burt's office, as I wanted to break all ties with Marius, his friends, and his family completely. I rented a very small office space measuring about 400 square feet in the centre of Castries. The place was big enough to accommodate a couple of desks, a couple of desktop computers, a printer, and a filing cabinet. It was there that I set up my office. I used the shop front to post brochures that contained photos and write-ups of properties that I was accumulating on my listings.

I met a man whilst working in my office, and we engaged in chatter as his eyes caught the postings on the window. It turned out that he had available a tiny, two-bedroom, one-bathroom apartment for rent. It was situated on the second floor of a three-storey building. I had soon arranged for the payment of one month's rent and one month as a security deposit, as is customary. The kitchen was impossible, only having one fitted, lower-level cupboard and absolutely no counter space. The windows throughout the apartment were stuck shut except for the one in the back bedroom, and there was little or no fresh air coming through. There were big spaces between the guardrails on the outside balcony, and there was nowhere for the children to play safely. I knew it would be a complete nightmare supervising them. This place was far from ideal, but it was affordable, and it would be my own place. At least I and the children would be away from Marius, and I would have peace of mind.

Although I had paid for the apartment, I was not sure how I was actually going to move my things out of the house, and this put me in quite a quandary for some days. I decided to move things out little by little by packing things and shifting them to the new place in my Jeep when Marius wasn't at home. I packed up things like pots and pans, vases, glasses, books, clothes, and floor rugs. I would bring things to the apartment after dropping the children to school in the morning and then head down to the office. On one particular morning, one of Marius' family members, who was living in a nearby house, observed me leaving the house in the Jeep when it was packed to the hilt. Later that day, she asked Marius if I was moving out. Up to that point, Marius had not even noticed that things were going missing in the house, but that evening, when he came home and looked around the house he had noticed the absence of many of the household items.

'Are you moving out, Hannah? I notice that you have taken away a lot of the things in the house.' I replied that I had found a place and that I was taking all of my possessions and my children with me. I asked him not to try to stop me as I had made up my mind that I was going. 'Oh, I will not stop you,' he said, 'and if you want me to help you to move, I can use the pickup truck to help you with the furniture.' I was completely taken aback at this seemingly kind offer as it was not at all what I expected his response to be once he found out. 'The only thing that I want you to do is to buy me a ticket to go to England so that I can start a new life there. I promise that I will not bother you as long as you buy a ticket for me.' I pondered this proposal for a few moments and rationalized that fair exchange was no robbery. It was a small price to pay for my freedom, my peace of mind, and my furniture, and so we quickly struck a deal and the whole 'break' was a lot simpler than I could have ever imagined.

~ ~ ~

Finally in my new apartment, I firmly closed the door behind me and slumped down onto the sofa. The children were fast asleep, and there was no loud music blaring from the sound systems of Marius' family members who would regularly blast it so loudly that the windows in our house would vibrate. The silence was deafening and only broken by the loud singing of the unseen crickets outside. As I sat in the chair in my new living room, I found myself weeping. A flood of emotions reached a crescendo inside my body. I wanted to laugh and sing and cry and scream all at the same time. 'I am free! I am free! Thank you, sweet Jesus, for this day. You have helped me to become free!' I sat there well into the night, just praising God and allowing myself to be enveloped in happiness and warmth and an incredible peace.

It was on one of these peaceful nights and not too long after I moved into the apartment, that I heard the voice of God speak to me. It was clear and it was firm and it was unmistakeable. As I sat on my grey leather sofa in my tiny living room, the Lord asked me to go and get a piece of paper and a pen. It was late, and I was feeling too comfortable to get up in search of the required items. I asked the Lord to just tell me what he had to say and that I would remember. The voice repeated its demand, and I then went off in search of the writing implements. When I found them, I returned to my seat. The Lord stated that I would be the founder of a residential home that would house spiritually and physically abused adolescent girls. The name of the home would be Heritage House, and it would be a safe haven for girls who were to be offered holistic recovery programmes to promote and provide educational, spiritual, emotional, and physical rehabilitation. I honestly did not know what to make of this particular encounter with God, or with the instructions that he asked me to write down, so I decided to speak to my pastor about it.

I explained to my pastor that I was just in the process of finding my own spiritual feet and that I was in no way ready to take on such a huge task. He reassured me that, if God indeed had given me the task, he would provide the way and the means for me to accomplish it, and that it might not necessarily be a task for immediate completion. He went on to say that it was more likely that God would ensure that I was settled emotionally and spiritually before he would allow me to embark on such an important journey to help others through their own misfortunes. I agreed with those sentiments and put the instructions and the encounter on the back burner of my mind.

CHAPTER 14

Finding Strength

It took quite some time for me to adjust to the fact that I was living alone with the kids. It was, of course, true that their biological father had seldom been around or done anything positive for the family, but my solitude was really brought home to me after we moved to another house altogether and I found myself the only person my children could rely on for everything . . . all of the time. I was not coping very well with the stress of a separation and moving house with two small children and also running a business that was less than a year old. I had to find new day care for Caleb that was closer to Castries, at a price that I could afford, and I also had enrol my daughter into kindergarten all at the same time.

School would open in September and so I asked Aunty Barbara, the owner of the cheapest day care in town, if she would possibly allow Hope to stay at the day care for the next three months until the new school term began. Aunty Barbara kindly obliged, but soon pointed out that she was not having difficulty with the baby but rather with Hope, my daughter. She soon noticed that Hope did not want to stay with the preschoolers, but much preferred to be with the younger toddlers. She would insist on crying and becoming clingy whenever she was taken to the section with the older children. She would beg me to leave her with Caleb. Huge tears would stream down her sad face. 'No, Mummy, no! Please let me stay here with Caleb. I don't want to go to the other side! Please, Mummy!'

Both the teachers and I were completely baffled by her behaviour, which repeated itself on a daily basis. It occurred to me one day that it was not just the first-day-at-school blues that many small children have and that something was deeply wrong. One morning after experiencing another one of these episodes, I decided to bend down and give her a hug and some comfort by squeezing her and patting her back gently. I asked Hope why she didn't want to go to the other side and play with the older children. 'Wouldn't that be more exciting for you?' I asked her. I felt both astonished and gutted when the little girl replied that if she was bad and didn't behave herself, then I would leave her like I left Daddy. So if she stayed with the baby she could see when I came for him and then I would be forced to take her with me as well. I think it was only then that I began to realize that, although my motives for leaving the house were reasonable, they still had a very negative effect on the children. The experience of the separation had traumatized them. I then knew that I had to constantly reassure them of my love and make sure they understood that they meant everything to me. I did my best, but admittedly it was very stressful and I sometimes failed.

I was able to enrol Hope into a private school where many of the well-to-do in Saint Lucian society sent their children. I wanted the best for my daughter and at the time believed that I was giving her a head start by ensuring her attendance there. Her first day at school was lovely, and I took photos of her in her neatly pressed uniform and perfectly styled hair. I remember the hairstyle quite plainly. It was called a cup and saucer, which was a single cornrow about an inch thick around the perimeter of her head and then a ponytail in the centre, which was finished off with a ribbon that matched the material of the school uniform. She was so pretty with her shiny black shoes and box-pleated skirt and cute dimples!

Soon, however, everything started to get on top of me. No money was coming in from anywhere, including the business, and I had taken on an assistant whom I had to pay for from my ever-depleting savings, which also financed the small office and sustained my family. After a few weeks, I no longer found time or energy to replace the buttons on Hope's uniform or comb her hair neatly. At times, I used small safety pins to hold the two sides of the uniform together. The buttonholes became torn, and holes soon appeared. My daughter's hair became *wassy*, which is Saint Lucian speak for unkempt or messy, and I felt powerless to do anything about it. It was a real chore to comb their hair. Caleb would scream and scream the house down as I attempted to moisturize, part, and comb his neck-length hair. Hope's hair was thicker and therefore even less manageable, and I undertook this monumental task of hairdressing as infrequently as I could. The children's appearance was just one of the many priorities that I had to think about, and finally it had sunk to the bottom of my list. It was not until her teacher asked to speak to me one afternoon as I was picking her up, that my heart automatically slumped and I dreaded what was to follow. I was pretty sure that I was in trouble with the teacher and that she was going to scold me as Hope looked particularly scruffy that day. 'Perhaps you know why I asked to see you? It's just that I have had to comb Hope's hair on occasions, and also her dress has got buttons missing!' I looked down at my daughter, and tears started to well up in my eyes. 'It is not good for her self-esteem,' continued the teacher. 'You understand, don't you'? I felt ashamed, embarrassed, and hurt on my daughter's behalf and wondered how I had managed to lose control of things. I apologized to the teacher and briefly told her of our circumstances and promised to try and do better in future. I brought the children home, fed and bathed them, and then put them to bed after a short while. It was in those quiet moments that I indulged myself in my thoughts, memories, self-pity, and the feeling of loneliness as warm tears streamed down my face.

It took me a whole year to close my first sale of a house. The commission was $10,000, and I was very excited, even though I had to wait for months to get paid whilst the mortgage was found and approved and documents were passed back and forth between the bank and the lawyers and the buyer and the seller. I got completely frustrated and whilst out on another unsuccessful viewing, decided to freak out whilst driving my assistant back to the office. My assistant attended the same church as I and was aware that I was attending deliverance sessions with the pastor. She became very concerned as I let it rip one afternoon after being let down by a client who had me going round and round on another wild goose chase. I cussed and snorted and cried all the way back to Castries from Balata, which was a few miles away. I was complaining about all sorts of things—the condition of my old, beat-up Jeep, the cost of petrol, the wasting of my time, the wasted phone calls relating to setting up dead-end appointments . . . and lots more besides.

I went home. After putting the kids to bed, I sat alone just staring at the wall in the living room. I was so angry and fed up with everything. I wondered why God wouldn't help me or heal my pain. Why was *everything* so difficult for me? I cried relentlessly for what seemed like hours, and a feeling of helplessness, exasperation, and darkness came over me. All sorts of thoughts raced through my mind, and with each one, I seemed to get angrier and angrier. I saw no point in continuing to go to church or serving God. After all, what good was it doing for me? I had little money left, no husband, a failed business, the sole responsibility for two small children, and heaps and heaps of bills. I wondered why my lot seemed to be worse than everyone else's, coupled with the fact that I thought that I was living a very clean life, but yet still I was plagued with this spiritual oppression. Why me?

My pastor had explained to me that I was suffering from a generational curse that had been handed down to me because of the iniquities of my forefathers. In my particular case, it was my actual parents who were the partakers of iniquity as they had routinely been involved in obeah rituals and practices. I never had anything to do with it, and never even gave it much thought except that I knew that it was wrong. I never knowingly participated in anything evil or contrary to the Bible, but apparently that does not matter. The word of God clearly states that the sins of the fathers are visited upon the children unto the third and fourth generation. That seemed hugely unfair to me, and I was fed up with being the fall guy for my parents or anyone else for that matter. How dare they ruin my life this way? My parents had eight children, and I was the youngest, so then why should I be the one to go through all of this? Shouldn't it have been the firstborn? I wondered if my parents had known what they were doing.

I remember asking Mum once why she could not just trust God for what she needed instead of being a slave to all of this evil. Mother matter-of-factly replied that she did trust in God, but yet she still had the right to help herself if she could! I came to understand that generational curses could in fact be broken through deep intercession, but I did not know exactly how long it would be before I would be totally free. What if it started to affect my own children? And what if I was to start manifesting demons whilst at home alone with them? Doom and gloom seemed to envelope me as complete despair seemed to capture my being. I wondered if I was acting the whole thing out. Maybe these things never actually happened and it was all in my imagination. Perhaps the church atmosphere and the emotion was what caused all of this to happen and it wasn't real. There was no other explanation for all of this stuff except that I had imagined the whole thing. I felt utterly confused and totally lost in a mishmash of emotion, fear, hurt, and desperation.

That evening at around nine thirty, I heard a knock at the front door. The voice was a familiar one, hoarse and strong and loud. 'Sister Hannah, are you in there? Open up the door please, it's your pastor here. I came to see how you are doing.' I froze momentarily and tried to collect my thoughts. I wondered if I had heard that right! Was Pastor at the door? I continued to stare at the wall on the opposite side of the room as I sat motionless and almost in a trance. 'Hannah, I know that you are in there. Come on and open up. We can see the lights on!' By now I knew that the voice was real, and I shifted heavily from the sofa to remove the bolts and latches from the front door. When I finally got the door open, I saw two familiar faces that were smiling at me, but I could also see concern in their eyes. Pastor said that he heard that I'd had a hard day and that he had come with his Armour Bearer to see if I was all right or needed assistance. I felt completely overwhelmed by their kind gesture, but was unable to answer.

The two men came in and sat down looking at me, but I could only answer their concern with loud sobs as I broke down in tears once more. I finally managed to blurt out complaint after complaint about how rough life was treating me. I explained my inability to cope and how emotionally tired I felt. Pastor listened carefully and spent time consoling me and using scriptures to show me that God was indeed there for me and that I should not give up. It was only natural for me to feel overwhelmed right now, he suggested, that I should read God's word as often as possible and keep singing his praise and worshipping him. He said that I should recite God's words over and over in my heart and—better still—say them out loud wherever possible. He said that I could fight back with the scriptures whenever the devil tried to break me. 'With every temptation, the Lord makes a way of escape.' Pastor proceeded to pray a very strong and inspirational prayer on my behalf asking the Lord to send ministering angels to my rescue and defence. He asked the Lord to cover me in his joy so that I would have the strength to cope with and overcome the challenges of life, such as the caring for the children, my business, and my loneliness. I was so incredibly uplifted by the time these two men of God left my home. As soon as they left, I went straight to my room and searched for the scriptures they asked me to read. I turned to Psalm 71. Verses 1-9 NIV

[1] In you, LORD, I have taken refuge;

let me never be put to shame.

[2] In your righteousness, rescue me and deliver me;

turn your ear to me and save me.

[3] Be my rock of refuge,

to which I can always go;

give the command to save me,

for you are my rock and my fortress.

[4] Deliver me, my God, from the hand of the wicked,

from the grasp of those who are evil and cruel.

[5] For you have been my hope, Sovereign LORD,

my confidence since my youth.

[6] From birth I have relied on you;

you brought me forth from my mother's womb.

I will ever praise you.

[7] I have become a sign to many;

you are my strong refuge.

[8] My mouth is filled with your praise,

declaring your splendor all day long.

[9] Do not cast me away when I am old;

do not forsake me when my strength is gone.

1

Before I started reading, I set the CD player to continuously repeat the beautiful strains of one of my favourite songs, *Praise Is What I Do*. It was written by William Murphy and these are my favourite lines:

I vow to praise you
Through the good and the bad
I'll praise you
Whether happy or sad

That night a deep peace overtook me, and I fell into a deep restful sleep whilst the words of the song sunk deep down into my spirit.

CHAPTER 15

The Blood, the Fire, and the Sword

Over the years I have found my pastor to be an invaluable resource to me; he was always on hand to provide me with spiritual support when I needed it. I have come to find that no matter what stage you are in your walk with God, two ingredients are *essential*—a good, bible-based, whole-gospel-preaching church, and a good pastor filled with the Holy Ghost I believe that if your church cannot change you, then you should change your church! And it may be useful to ask yourself if your pastor possesses the following basic characteristics that are necessary for him or her to have in order to be able to shepherd the flock effectively:

Encouragement

A good pastor must be able to encourage and support his members in their times of need. Remember, to whom much is given, much is required, and this is one of the first and most serious responsibilities . . . that of jealously guarding the flock.

Jeremiah 23:1-4 (NIV) tells us:

> [1] 'Woe to the shepherds who are destroying and scattering the sheep of my pasture!' declares the Lord. [2] Therefore this is what the Lord, the God of Israel, says to the shepherds who tend my people: 'Because you have scattered my flock and driven them away and have not bestowed care on them, I will bestow punishment on you for the evil you have done,' declares the Lord. [3] 'I myself will gather the remnant of my flock out of all the countries where I have driven them and will bring them back to their pasture, where they will be fruitful and increase in number. [4] I will place shepherds over them who will tend them, and they will no longer be afraid or terrified, nor will any be missing,' declares the Lord.

Faith

A good pastor should be a person of faith who can demonstrate from a personal perspective how faith in God can move the mountains in the life of each member, and bring the scriptures alive by illustrating the Holy Word and showing how these things can become a reality.

Acts 11:23 and 24 (NIV) explains:

> [23] When he arrived and saw what the grace of God had done, he was glad and encouraged them all to remain true to the Lord with all their hearts. [24] He was a good man, full of the

Holy Spirit and faith, and a great number of people were brought to the Lord.

Light

A pastor should be able to shine like a beacon of hope to his followers. He should be a man beyond reproach and of good standing, not only in public but in the secret and hidden places also.

Mathew 5:15 (NIV) says: 'In the same way, let your light shine before men, that they may see your good deeds and praise your Father in heaven.'

Comfort

All believers go through different seasons in their lives and will need the comforting listening ear of the pastor. For some people, nothing else will do but to be able to pour out their pain and sorrow to one of the most trusted and beloved persons in their life. Remember, scripture tells us that even Jesus Christ our Lord was sent ministering angels to comfort him in his darkest hours!

Matthew 4:11 (NIV) reminds us: 'Then the devil left, him and angels came and attended him.'

Availability

The shepherd must always be available to his sheep or make provision for them to be cared for if it is not possible for him to do so personally. Just like newborn babies who make high demands on the parents, some church members will be needy; but as they grow older and wiser, they will learn to be more independent and will therefore require less attention. Some pastors have lost their ability to care for their flocks, which is demonstrated by their lack of awareness when members are hurting, sick, missing, spiritually comatose, or spiritually dead. Pastors have a responsibility to visit their members on a periodic basis at their homes and pray with them and their families. If the church is very large, then I believe that some sort of schedule should be made for home visits, personal counselling, or some kind of one-on-one interaction, preferably with the pastor or his or her immediate leadership team. Sometimes all it takes is a warm smile and a gentle handshake, a pat on the back, or a quick phone call to encourage a soul, but alas, even this can be hard to find in the body of Christ at times as people rush to the comfort of their cliques. I do not think that I would have survived if it had not been for the love and support of my pastor, whom I once found at the end of the phone in the early hours of the morning!

We can read about how the boy Samuel made himself available to do the Lord's work in Samuel Chapter 3. The spiritual welfare of the members in the church should be of paramount importance to not only the pastor, but the whole membership, and we have a duty to extend love and support to every person but especially to the members of the body of Christ. If the church is truly a refuge, then we need to take personal responsibility for the sheep left in our charge so that they do not go astray because of lack of care. So many ministries seem to concentrate more and more of their efforts on the sowing of seed and prosperity and giving, often making members bitter and sometimes offended about how much money they sow into the ministry whilst by the same token not being able to receive the support and love that they so desperately need. This can be is very disappointing. I believe that tithing and giving is scriptural and it supports and is a necessary part of the work of the church ministry. I do not believe that sowing seed is just about money; we can also sow seeds of love, hope, and trust in all those who enter into the House of the Lord.

Over the years that followed, I wanted to find out more and more about the Lord Jesus and the spirit realm so I joined a school of ministry that was run by my local church. The course of study lasted for two academic years. It was an opportunity to sit in a class with other students and learn about the Bible, God's power, his will, and also ask lots of questions. The classes were really interesting and exciting, and we had different tutors who taught various topics. We were engaged in group activities and also worked on our own to produce assignments and practical sessions at other churches where we students were given almost complete charge of the services. I seemed to have an unquenchable yearning to find out more about the spirit realm and especially why I have manifested demons over the years. I wanted to know how I could be free from them once and for all.

Isaiah 59 is a powerful chapter, but verse 19 is particularly meaningful to me (KJV): 'So shall they fear the name of the Lord from the west, and his glory from the rising of the sun. When the enemy shall come in like a flood, the Spirit of the Lord shall lift up a standard against him.'

Demons can remain dormant and undetected in a person for many years, but once they have been given entrance into a person's life through an open door, they will cause havoc in every area. They will silently orchestrate your thought patterns, behaviour, and speech. They will tell you what to do and when to do it. They will speak to your mind and make you say all sorts of things. They can also control your body so that you do what they want. After one of these episodes, I would feel thoroughly embarrassed and ashamed at the spectacle I had caused, even though I knew I had absolutely no control over what had happened. Only the blood of Jesus can deliver a person from demonization, and although demons can control your body—arms and legs when you are manifesting for example—they cannot enter into the soul of a born-again believer.

I said earlier that demons unwillingly manifest themselves, and I believe that most times this is actually true. I believe this because, if you think about it, no one would willingly run the risk of being evicted from a very comfortable home that they have lived in and are quite happy in. A person's body is the perfect habitat for demons, and they would much prefer to stay there indefinitely and undetected. However, when demons are in an anointed atmosphere or in the presence of a person who has the anointing of God, it can become very uncomfortable for them. Unseen spiritual warfare takes place between God and those demonic forces that are found to be present in that person's body, and the demons are forcibly ejected.

It is worth mentioning here that the deliverance ministers who are praying with somebody should always remember that they are dealing with an actual person with real feelings of pain. Therefore when restraining a person to prevent them from hurting themselves or others, we should always be mindful of the pressure and force used. Demons don't care about the individual they enter, and so during manifestations, they can cause the person to hurt himself, herself, or others through violent outbursts. Excessive force such as the pulling of hair, placing the arm behind the back, or slapping should never be used. There have been some dreadful stories over the years of terrible injuries and even accidental deaths during deliverance. Demons are spirits and cannot be harmed by physical force. The word of God explains this clearly to us in Ephesians 6:12 (KJV): 'For we wrestle not against flesh and blood, but against principalities, against powers, against the rulers of the darkness of this world, against spiritual wickedness in high places.'

Evil spirits love to give a display of their prowess and also to control the environment. They can often bring new meaning to the phrase 'show stopper' if they are not put under immediate subjection and control. In these situations, the ministers must assert their authority through the name of Jesus Christ of Nazareth and immobilize and subdue the demon spirit inside the person, remembering always that it is not the actual person who is deliberately being disruptive, but the demons that have unwillingly manifested themselves within that person.

On one particular occasion I visited a church where the pastor spent the evening teaching about the dunamis, or power, that Jesus delegated to the apostles and how this was used to do many miraculous works. At the end of the service, all those gathered were asked to hold either money or their bank cards in their hands so that the pastor could pray on each person's finances individually. There were probably close to about sixty people in the room at the time, and they were seated in two rows on either side of the church. The pastor started praying for people from the front of the far side of the room first, working his way up from the back of the second row to the front again. I was seated approximately four rows from the front in the near-side row. I noticed that when he started to pray for me, he held the hand holding my bank cards in his. He started praying, but then he started to see into the spirit realm and he began to explain various things that he discerned concerning me. Soon, however, I started to move and gyrate and struggle away from him, but his grip was firm. The next thing I noticed was that I had started to manifest and disrupt the whole service.

At the time of this event, I had divorced Marius some years earlier and was remarried to a very wonderful and spirit-filled man. By that time, I and the children were living with my new husband in a new family home and we had started to attend another pentecostal assembly which was closer to us and where my husband preached regularly. Upon arriving home that Sunday night, I explained to him what had happened and he comforted me and prayed with me for the peace of God to caress me, and for his joy to give me strength. I found a tower of strength in my husband, and his warm strong arms and soft comforting words reassured me as I embarked on a broken night of sleep. The following week was hard and long, and I tried to be strong, but fell back into a slump when I noticed people doing double takes as I walked past them in the city of Castries. I no longer wanted to go out of the house as I felt that people were looking at me and judging me. In all honesty, who could blame them? I believed that people must have thought that I was a witch; it was all very hard indeed. As the week drew to a close, I looked forward to going into the house of God on Sunday morning hoping to find solace there. When the day finally arrived, I took part in the praise and worship and sat and listened to the sermon, which was entitled 'Expose and Expel.'

The pastor spoke about devils in the church and ravenous wolves hiding amongst the sheep waiting to devour them. He spoke of the devil being subtle and how Christians must be vigilant in seeking them out and exposing them and then getting rid of them. When the service ended, the two pastors present called my husband and I to a meeting at the front of the church. They explained to my husband that they had received a report concerning my attendance at another church the previous Sunday where I had manifested demons and caused chaos in the service. One of the pastors then made eye contact with me and addressed me for the first and only time during that meeting by asking me if I had told my husband what had transpired. My heart began to race and I could feel its thud, thud, thud in my temple. I replied that he was sitting right in front of him, so he should ask him. At this point my husband confirmed that he knew about the incident. I wondered to myself what repercussions could have developed in my relationship with my husband if I had not told him of the unfortunate incident before that impromptu meeting was called. I felt that the pastors obviously never cared about that, as they fervently felt that they were doing God's work, and now that I was exposed, I should be expelled. One of the pastors stated that. this type of behaviour could not be tolerated by the Church. The pastors told my husband that, as the head of the household, he would have to take responsibility for my actions, and therefore he was thereby indefinitely suspended from preaching or participating in any ministry duty.

We sat there in complete silence and incredulity for the sum total of the four minutes that the meeting took. The pastors told us they had been made aware of the situation by a church sister. They believed that incident was not the first time that I had manifested demons, and so I should go to see Pastor McLorren at Bethel Tabernacle Church for deliverance. With that statement, the pastors dismissed both of us. My husband and I got up from our seats and walked away in silence. Bitter tears stung my face as I silently rehearsed the now-familiar song in which I had come to find incredible comfort: 'How Great Ia Our God', written by Chris Tomlin

> **The splendor of the King**
> **Clothed in majesty**
> **Let all the earth rejoice**
> **All the earth rejoice**

~ ~ ~

The church sister the pastor referred to was, in fact, a close confidant of mine who was a senior member of the church that I had visited that day. She must have been so eager to answer that she knew me when the pastor enquired about me that night. We used to visit each other at home and share intimate secrets, talk, and laugh together. All of a sudden, she was my betrayer I thought, giving away personal information—who I was and what church I attended and more. This information enabled the attending pastor from that night to track down the pastors of my own assembly and report me to them.

I can remember that just before our pastors confronted my husband and me, she abruptly stopped taking my phone calls, so I tried calling with a hidden number to establish if she was avoiding me. True to form, she picked up those calls.

When I confronted her, she made some feeble excuse about her phone not working properly, but I soon got the message that she no longer wanted to speak to me. We used to e-mail and text and attend classes together and speak about our families and our future. She was a single mum, and I happily had given her advice on some of the ways I had overcome loneliness as a Christian single woman. I asked myself, Why? Why? How could she do this to me? I remember asking her to give me an opportunity to put right anything I had done to offend her, but she said only that I had not done anything wrong. I noted that the time that she stopped talking to me was immediately after we were praying together one day and I had manifested. The loss of my friend felt like a bereavement. I surmised that it would be best to limit my friends from then on and concentrate my efforts more on my own family instead to avoid such betrayal in the future.

On the night of the terrible incident, I sent a text message to the pastor to say that I had arrived home safely, but I never received a reply. On the following morning, I called the pastor and apologized for the incident and asked if I could meet with him to talk. But the pastor told me that he was not prepared to deal with cases such as mine. He explained that he didn't own his own church building and could not accommodate any further meetings with me. He quickly dismissed me and told me to go and see Pastor McLorren who would be able to help me. I then pleaded with the pastor for an opportunity to speak to him about what had happened and asked for some time to perhaps receive some counselling, but the conversation came to an abrupt end after I asked him if he was pushing me away, to which he simply replied that he was not, but he was unable to help me.

I cannot adequately convey the sheer magnitude of the rejection that I felt in those moments and the weeks and months that followed. No words could express the tsunami currents of deep hurt and stinging humiliation that ripped through my being. I wanted to die. I imagined myself driving to Pigeon Island Beach very early in the morning and walking into the sea until my feet no longer touched the ground. I would be gently swept away into eternity where I would no longer hurt. Deep down I knew that this thought in itself was a sin, and I was forced by my conscience to dismiss it. I wondered why God had forsaken me and what I had done to deserve all of this. I felt less than worthless, and I wanted to disappear. My darling husband certainly did not deserve to be ostracized because of me, and I wondered if it was even biblical for the pastors to use me as a big stick and ban my husband from the pulpit as they had done in such a merciless way.

What struck me most was the lack of love, compassion, and understanding in the whole matter. I have never to this day been asked about my version of events, or how I felt, or if I needed any type of support. The apparently overzealous pastors seemed to disregard the fact that Christ never punished anyone he ministered to, but instead showed compassion and patience and love.

The memory of this banishment lasted for a very long time, and I prayed and had to repent for the initial animosity that I felt against the pastors for the way in which both my husband and I were treated. In time, I learnt to forgive the pastors as I understood that their knowledge was limited, and that when they acted, they believed that they were doing the right thing. It was the beginning of a tremendous learning curve for me, as the Lord revealed to me very forcefully that doors in my spirit life had been opened because of my disobedience and lack of respect for my own pastor. The Holy Spirit warned me on many occasions to stop speaking ill against a man whom I felt was inept, biased, and lacked anointing. I had little respect for him because of the way in which he had conducted himself, and I also thought that he lacked integrity. I made no excuses for the verbal attacks that I regularly launched in his direction, despite the Lord's cautioning me to desist from the practice.

During the period after the incident, the Holy Spirit revealed to me that pride had entered into my life, and the Lord had chosen to severely rebuke me by permitting the manifestation that occurred that day. Humility became my first name after that as my entire soul was laid bare for all to see, and I became nothing before my own eyes and also in the eyes of many. God showed me scriptures relating to Miriam who was the sister of Moses and how she challenged his authority. I was made to understand that it was not for me to fight, challenge, or disrespect my pastor even if he was not acting in the will of God. My duty as a child of God was to pray and remain respectful. I learnt a painful but important lesson—we need to honour those who have the rule over us even though we may inwardly not agree with them. This does not, however, mean that we should tolerate abuse or that we should commit sin or do anything that is against our Christian conscience. God hates pride as it is the opposite of humility, and I understand very clearly now the scripture that says, 'For whom the Lord loves he chastens' (Hebrews 12:6, KJV). Deep wounds and deep hurts can arise from the mismanagement of situations within the body of Christ. These types of wounds are often the most difficult to heal as the House of God is supposed to be a place of refuge and help and comfort. If we are not careful, it can cause the weak to give up the race as they fall away in discouragement and despair.

All those who point the finger at others for having been oppressed by demons should ask themselves if they have any characteristics of demons themselves. The first reaction would be that everyone would say, of course not, but if we look a little closer for a moment, we can see that pride is a trait derived from Leviathan, an extremely powerful marine spirit. It is interesting to note that pride can be found in many of us, and we sing songs all the time asking for the Lord to break us and mould us on his potter's wheel into what he wants us to be. But do we consider that we personally need deliverance because we are proud? What about the inability to forgive someone for something we perceive he or she has done to us so many years ago? Can we relate to the emotions of unforgivingness, anger, hatred, vengeance, depression, or stress? What about the little lies that we tell from time to time? Do we know or acknowledge that demon spirits are the ones that persuade us to deceive, lie, and commit sexual sins? If we find ourselves doing these things, we need deliverance just like those whom we consider to be workers of iniquity. The spirit of fear is also an extremely powerful demon. Who amongst us will admit to ever being afraid? 1 John 4:18 (KJV): 'There is no fear in love; but perfect love casteth out fear: because fear hath torment. He that feareth is not made perfect in love.'

The word of God clearly refers to fear as being a demon that should be cast out. So we can see clearly that we should not only think of witches and wizards as being the only ones who need deliverance. We all need to examine ourselves daily and ask the Lord to purge us thoroughly from everything that will hinder us from entering heaven.

I learnt that sickness too can be cast out in the precious name of Jesus and that children of the Most High God do not have to tolerate infirmity, which is an evil spirit. I had been suffering from the symptoms of uterine fibroids over the period of about a year, and frequently likened myself to the woman in the Bible who was suffering with the issue of blood. There were times when I dared not leave the house because of the excruciating pain or because the flow was so heavy. It got so bad that I became anaemic. On one occasion I actually collapsed whilst attending Sunday morning service because I was so weak and dizzy. The emergency room doctor ordered me to go home and rest and take iron supplements.

After confirming that I had multiple fibroids and starting me on a regimen of hormones to ebb the nonstop flow, the gynaecologist I was consulting at the time recommended the complete removal of my uterus. Unfortunately, the flow persisted and I started to become very concerned indeed about my health and decided to get a second opinion from a doctor at a local private hospital. After taking a full medical history, the new doctor immediately did a biopsy of my uterine tissue. The results indicated that, although the tissue was benign, I had severe inflammation and large fibroids. She also recommended the removal of the uterus. She stated that since I already had two caesarean section operations for the birth of my children, she was not prepared to just 'go in and remove the offending tissue' in case it decided to grow back again. She tripled the dose of the hormone medication and put me on even stronger painkillers so that I could get through the days and nights more comfortably, but the flow was still constant. The idea of the complete removal of my womb was not a favourable one at all, I later found out by researching online that the hormones that I was given were actually birth control tablets and this made me very angry considering that I had repeatedly explained to the doctors that it was my hope to have another child. I thought at least that they should have explained to me that it was a hormone contraceptive that I was being given which would have given me my right to decide whether or not I wanted to proceed to take them.

As the date for surgery was approaching, we sought God's face in earnest. This situation led my husband to embark on a long journey of fasting and deep intercession. At first it was a twenty-one day fast, then a seven-day fast and a series of mini fasts. All during the following months I felt emotionally drained wondering if I should undergo the surgery or not. I regularly went up on the healing line at church to be prayed for, but alas I had no reprieve.

My despondence regarding the whole situation finally led me to feel resigned about my fate, but my husband continued to fast and pray. He wanted me to have either a successful surgery or preferably no surgery at all. In the midst of all of this, my eleven-year-old son reported to me that he had a dream that he saw an evil looking man operating on me in the hospital. His dream was coupled with my own dreams and constant thoughts that I would not survive the surgery. On one particular night I saw myself in my bedroom looking out towards the balcony where there were around six large black dogs just prowling back and forth. Above their heads were a flock of large black birds going round and round in the sky above. In the dream I immediately began to pray and call forth thunder and lightening from heaven to strike and consume them. Whilst praying, I beheld flashes of light and sparks of flame attacking the dogs and the birds until they finally disappeared. My husband also had dreams that the surgery would not go well, and had become not a little agitated, waking up at three a.m to command the morning as outlined in Job chapter 38 12 KJV: asking God for a breakthrough. As the date of the date of the surgery loomed closer and closer, I felt as if I could no longer function as a wife or mother, and things reached breaking point.

I can remember that I called a family meeting. I explained that I felt that no one cared about how I felt and that they were unsympathetic to my plight. I went on to list the emotional and physical turmoil that I was in. I explained that I felt that I was going to die if I had the surgery, but had no alternative because of my physical state. It was at this point that my husband asked me if I had done what he had asked me to do some months earlier. I actually had no idea what he was referring to, so he had to remind me that he had asked me to give an amount of money to the church that was equal to the cost of the surgery. I remembered his request, but told him that there was no point in doing that as I was still having symptoms. He then went on to explain that, during his nights of intercession, God had revealed to him that I should sow a seed offering on behalf of my health and also stop taking the medication that I was on. Quite frankly, I was reluctant to accede to this request, but the children joined in unison insisting that I sow the seed and stop taking the medication. Because of everyone's enthusiasm, I felt that I had no choice but to relent to both parts of the petition.

By that evening, the pain reached an unbearable crescendo, and I screamed throughout the night in sheer agony. At times I would sit up, then lie down, then walk around. I would lie on the floor, crouch, then double over, but I found no rest for the entire night. My husband kept the night vigil with me and prayed and rubbed my tummy and aggressively commanded the demons of sickness inside to leave my body. By half past five in the morning, the birds were in full chorus as I reached for the painkillers, which finally allowed me to sleep. Over the next few days, my husband stayed with me—day and night—in serious warfare prayer whilst giving me a simple concoction of olive oil, water, and salt to drink saying that it was a point of contact for his prayers for my healing. I noticed that each successive night the pain was reduced from the night before. I was still taking the painkillers when necessary, but not the hormones, which hadn't completely ebbed the flow anyway. After the fifth day, I noticed that I was no longer in any kind of pain so I stopped taking the painkillers completely. As each day passed, the flow became lighter and lighter until, by day seventeen, the bleeding completely stopped. Hallelujah!

The date for surgery soon arrived, but we knew, deep down in our hearts, that God had come through for us and there would be no need to go through with the procedure. We decided to attend the hospital on the morning anyway to explain to the doctors that I no longer had symptoms and would therefore not be undergoing the surgery. The consultant became not a little upset saying that she was no longer prepared to treat me if I refused to be admitted and that she would refer me to see some other doctor. She asked us not to contact her again because we were wasting her time and that she would update my hospital file to that effect! We explained that we had fasted and prayed and that the Lord had answered our prayers and healed me completely and that no doctor would share the glory with God in the healing of my body. Up to this day, I have felt none of the pain that I suffered with for over a year. And I have felt no other symptoms as the seed that was planted for my health germinated quickly and led to the expulsion of the spirit of infirmity that was causing the sickness in my body!

The Lord has also given us many lethal weapons to fight with when engaged in spiritual warfare, and these are all made available to us through the scriptures. I have outlined some of them here:

- The Blood of Jesus Christ is the most potent of all weapons as it represents our covering and our protection against counter attack. When used directly against the enemy, it cannot be resisted.
- The all-consuming Fire of God—Hebrews 12:29 For our God is a consuming fire and nothing can withstand or quench this as it destroys everything in it's path.
- The Sword of the Spirit, which is the word of God and is sharper than a two edged sword which can destroy even the strongest demon.
- The anointing—Can be defined as the power of God made manifest in an individual by the Holy Spirit to do His will.
- Praying and worshiping in tongues This can be either tongues of men or heavenly tongues but both are used as a prayer language and directed to God. The enemy cannot intercept this weapon and it should be used freely when in battle.
- Using the name of Jesus Christ of Nazareth—At the name of Jesus every knee must bow and submit as it is all powerful.

- Binding and loosing—This is used to restrain the influence of Satan over your life or over the lives of your loved ones and to separate yourself from anything that is not beneficial to you.
- The full arsenal as found in Psalm 35 A very powerful array of weapons used for a full onslaught attack.
- Ambush and confusion—Tactical prowess catches the enemy off guard and gives the angelic hosts the advantage.
- Divine carpenters, hunters, fishers, and ravenous birds These weapons are released by The Lord to hunt and deal with hidden demons wherever they are. The divine fishers operate in the marine world while the hunters operate on land. Jeremiah 16 16-17. The ravenous birds of Isaiah 46:11 are like scavengers eating the flesh of the enemy.
- Chariots of fire—2 Kings 6:617 and Isaiah 66:15-16—You can use this weapon when you are attacked by a whole army from the camp of the enemy.
- Mighty warring angels with their swords drawn—The warring angels go into active combat with demonic forces on our behalf and we can command them to fight on our behalf.
- The east wind—which is used to scatter and send your enemy into confusion as described in Isiah 41:6 and psalm 48:6,7
- Flying rolls—as outlined in Zecharia 5:2 which are commanded to go forth to recover stolen property which has been taken by the enemy. This can be lost sales, a marriage, a promotion on the job finances or, your spiritual star as in Mathew:2 1,2
- Prayer and fasting—Certain stubborn spirits such as marine spirits need a more aggressive approach before they can be cast out and a season of prayer and fasting and reading God's word will assist greatly in this process.

Spiritual discernment is a most important key, and the Christian warrior must be on the offensive to spoil the plans of the devil and his kingdom. When we are engaged in warfare, we must be bold and strong. We must rest assured that the Lord our God is with us as he takes his position as Captain of the Hosts. He is mighty in battle and our strong deliverer, our refuge, and a very present help in the time of trouble. As soldiers of the cross, we rest assured that we have stronger and more valiant warriors on our side, and as the battle rages on, the companies of angels in heaven fall down in the sheer ecstasy of worship. The angelic hosts stand in unison to sing the timeless masterpiece of ultimate praise accompanied by the heavenly full orchestra to the King!

> For the lord God omnipotent reigneth
> Hallelujah hallelujah hallelujah hallelujah
> For the lord God omnipotent reigneth
> Hallelujah hallelujah hallelujah hallelujah
> For the lord God omnipotent reigneth
> Hallelujah hallelujah hallelujah hallelujah

MOTTO

Come, ye children, hearken unto me: I will teach you the fear of the LORD. Psalm 34;11kjv

The Lord gave me a vision way back in 2002. He told me he wanted me to open a safe haven for hurting adolescent young girls. He instructed that the home should be called Heritage House and should be a place of refuge and of hope for girls aged between eleven and eighteen years.

Since the time that I had this vision, it has stayed on the back burner as, although many are impressed with the concept, we have lacked sufficient practical and financial assistance in the venture so far.

The Mission Statement of the Home is that we will provide . . .

A sanctuary for children where they can receive shelter, food, clothing, nurturing, and spiritual enrichment.

A place where children can be mentored and cherished, where they receive scholarships, and learn about Christian values.

A holistic nurturing approach will be adopted including activities such as taking holidays, going to church, and learning to form a productive part of a family unit.

We are committed:

* *To provide a place of safety, learning, comfort and happiness.*
* *To provide a place of relaxation and fun, a refuge from cruelty and abuse.*
* *To provide a place where children can be loved and also learn how to love.*
* *To provide a place where children can get to know the love of the Lord.*
* *To provide a place where children can receive counselling and rehabilitation.*
* *To provide a place where life skills are taught and skills will be acquired to become a successful member of the community.*
* *To provide a place of cleanliness, a beacon of hope and a sanctuary for God's heritage*

If you would like to donate towards the establishment of this home, please visit our website at www.heritagehouseinstlucia.org for more information.

Lightning Source UK Ltd.
Milton Keynes UK
UKOW05f0743180813

215530UK00003B/442/P